THE KILLING OF MELISSA MAHON

AND THE TRIAL OF RONNIE DUNBAR

Bronagh Murphy

Gill & Macmillan

Gill & Macmillan Ltd
Hume Avenue, Park West, Dublin 12
with associated companies throughout the world
www.gillmacmillan.ie

© Bronagh Murphy 2009
978 07171 4749 6

Print origination by O'K Graphic Design, Dublin
Printed in the UK by CPI Cox and Wyman

This book is typeset in10/12.5 pt Minion

The paper used in this book comes from the wood pulp of
managed forests. For every tree felled, at least one tree is
planted, thereby renewing natural resources.

A CIP catalogue record for this book is available from the
British Library.

5 4 3 2 1

For Rita and Bobby

CONTENTS

01 | A GRUESOME DISCOVERY

The gruesome discovery of human remains at Lough Gill near Parkes Castle in County Leitrim in February 2008 marked the unravelling of the horrifying fate of Melissa Mahon. She had disappeared nearly 17 months earlier and, despite extensive appeals and investigations, gardaí had failed to locate her and no useful intelligence about what had happened to the 14-year-old schoolgirl had been uncovered. A missing-person investigation was ongoing when detectives finally received an unprompted phone call in which a troubled 16-year-old girl made shocking allegations against her father and, a day later, led gardaí to a secluded spot along the River Bonet where she claimed her father had dumped her friend's lifeless body.

Melissa was last seen in Sligo town on 14 September 2006. In the weeks following her disappearance, the national newspapers published her photograph and requests for information were made, as fears for the girl mounted. Melissa's mother, Mary Mahon, made an emotional appeal during which she choked back tears as she pleaded with her youngest child to, 'Please come home, my darling. I won't let anyone harm you.'

The press described Melissa as a 'vulnerable' girl. She had been born in England and had lived in London until the year before her disappearance. She was five feet tall, of slight build, thin, pale and with long, dark hair. During her appeal, Melissa's mother told the press that she did not know why the teenager would have gone away. There had been talk that Melissa may have run off with a boy her own age, but her mother did not believe this claim.

A year earlier, Mary Mahon had moved herself, her husband, Frederick, and their ten children back to her home town amid fears for her daughters' safety. 'Where we lived in London was getting dangerous and girls could get raped or anything,' she told the *Irish Mirror*. However, after Melissa's disappearance, Mary changed her mind about the security she had thought Sligo would offer, 'I blame this town for what happened to her. She is very young and she just could not cope with all this new-found freedom.'

By November 2006, Melissa had been missing for two months and gardaí made a fresh appeal for information. A garda spokesman said, 'She is a young girl and obviously to vanish like this is of grave concern to many people.' A reconstruction of Melissa's last known movements was filmed and broadcast on RTÉ's 'CrimeCall' programme, but proved to be of no benefit to the investigation.

Gardaí received reports of sightings of Melissa in Sligo and Athlone during this period, but the ensuing investigations all led to dead ends. She had seemingly vanished without a trace.

Melissa's 15th birthday fell on 10 March 2007, six months after she had last been seen. Gardaí again appealed in the national press for information and, this time, reports were made of sightings in Roscommon and Cork, but, again, investigations came to naught.

A year after Melissa's disappearance, police were no closer to discovering what had become of her. Mary Mahon again spoke to the press and told the *Sligo Weekender* that her daughter was a quiet girl who liked country-and-western music. It was reported that a teenage boy had been interviewed by police and had been described by gardaí as 'helpful' but he, too, had been unable to shed any light on where Melissa might be.

Inspector Paul Cuttle used the media to send a message to

Melissa. He wanted her to know that she was not in any trouble and that she should get in touch as soon as possible to assure gardaí and her family that she was safe and well.

As Melissa had been born and raised in England, a theory developed that she might have returned there. Gardaí contacted police in the United Kingdom and alerted ports and airports but, again, nothing new was learned.

In December 2007, Detective Inspector John O'Reilly, who was to become the chief investigating officer in the inquiry into Melissa's murder, made what was to be their final appeal for information, saying, 'We are sending this renewed appeal in the run-up to Christmas which can be a very lonely time for families. We want the message to get across that we are still actively seeking this little girl and anyone with information, however innocuous, should come forward.' Six weeks later, the long-awaited lead finally arrived.

In Sligo, on Thursday, 31 January 2008, a young father came home to find his teenage girlfriend and her younger teenage sister in highly distressed states. The girls were screaming and crying and as soon as he learned why they were so upset, he rang the local garda station and asked to speak to a detective. Gardaí arrived at his house shortly afterwards and, after hearing what the two had to say, took all three to Sligo Garda Station to make statements.

The following morning, Detective Inspector Colm Nevin and Detective Sergeant Con Lee met the two sisters, Samantha and Shirley Dunbar, at the Sligo Park Hotel. As they were aged 16 and 17, a social worker, Hilary Mullen, was also present.

They went over what had happened the previous evening, when Samantha had finally broken down and admitted to Shirley that she and their younger sister knew what had happened to Melissa Mahon. She said that, in September 2006, they had watched their father, Ronald Dunbar, kill Melissa and then had helped him dump her body in a river.

Hilary Mullen would later tell the Central Criminal Court that Samantha and her younger sister had been referred to her in February 2006 and that she had dealt closely with them. Until

1 February 2008, Samantha had never said a word to her about Melissa's disappearance and a mere six weeks before Samantha made her statement to gardaí, the younger girl had also behaved as though she knew nothing. She had seen a newspaper article that had referred to a sighting of Melissa and had said to Hilary Mullen, 'That's good, isn't it?', as though she was no wiser than anyone else.

The detectives, Samantha, Shirley and Hilary Mullen left the hotel in a patrol car at 11 a.m. on a wet Friday morning. They travelled to the girls' former home in the Rathbraughan Estate, where Ronnie Dunbar still lived. The girls had not lived with their father for some time and their younger sister was in the care of the Health Service Executive.

Samantha was asked to indicate the route that her father had taken from the house on the day she claimed he had killed Melissa and disposed of her body. She pointed out the way as they drove for 25 minutes, taking the Clarion and Dromahair roads into County Leitrim. They passed Parkes Castle and turned off the main road to drive down a narrow lane towards the River Bonet. When they had driven as far as they could, Samantha led the detectives on foot to a clearing at the edge of the water. She told them that this was the place where Melissa's body had been dumped. Garda subaqua teams were immediately dispatched to begin a search of the area.

The painstaking operation required members of the garda search team to form a straight line of four men along a rope that ran from the riverbank into the water. As they slowly edged forwards, they meticulously scoured the ground and water for evidence of a body or its remains. If and when a member of the team spotted an item of interest, they would tug the rope indicating to the others to stop.

The search of the muddy riverbanks and bed began at the spot Samantha had indicated. It then followed the flow of the river towards Lough Gill. The length of the river was examined in the early days of February 2008 but yielded nothing. The search was frustrated by poor weather conditions and was suspended on 4 February because of heavy rain. It began afresh on 8 February and moved away from the River Bonet and, by 11 February, on to the shoreline of Lough Gill.

Garda David Finn from the Athlone Water Unit was a member of the underwater search team from 9 to 14 February. At 2 p.m. on 11 February, he found a large bone fragment at the lake's shore around 200 metres from the mouth of the river. It was part of a human skull. Later that day, further bone fragments and five human teeth were found in the same vicinity.

The following morning, Garda Daniel Murphy was walking along the lake's edge adjacent to the area where the bones had been found. He was in the water up to his knees and held the end of the rope on to which the other divers were attached. In front of him, in one foot of water, he saw a lower jaw bone. He pulled the rope to stop the other searchers. A diver who was farther into the lake looked towards the shore and spotted white objects to the right of Garda Murphy. They were human bones. The search team had found the main area where the remains of Melissa were washed up. Then, beside a large rock under a tree, they found a child's nightdress, a sleeping bag and a man's neck tie. What was found along the shoreline tallied with the information that 16-year-old Samantha had given to gardaí.

A murder investigation was under way. The story of how Melissa Mahon, young and vulnerable, was abandoned by those who should have protected her and then lost her life in the most sordid of circumstances was about to be told.

02 | TWO FAMILIES RETURN

It was perhaps unsurprising that Melissa Mahon and Samantha Dunbar would gravitate towards one another and become friends during the academic year of 2005 to 2006. Both girls had been born and raised in England, and so had English accents, and both had recently been moved to their respective parents' home town of Sligo. Thirteen-year-old Melissa and her 15-year-old sister, Leeanna, started school at the Mercy College in September 2005 and soon met the three Dunbar girls. Fifteen-year-old Shirley Dunbar was nine months older than her then 14-year-old sister, Samantha. Their younger sister had turned 13 at the start of that school year. As she cannot be named in this book for legal reasons, she will be referred to as Jill, which is not her real name.

Jill and Melissa were in the same class at school and started to hang around together. Samantha was initially suspicious of the friendship but, eventually, warmed to her sister's slightly built, pretty friend. Whether it was Melissa who was a bad influence on Samantha and Jill, or vice versa, depends on whose version of events is being told. Frederick Mahon believes that his daughter was doing fine in school until she made her new friends. According to him, it was only after meeting the Dunbar girls that

Melissa started playing truant and getting into trouble. Samantha, on the other hand, said that she had not liked Melissa at first because she had been encouraging Jill to get into trouble. Despite Samantha's reservations, a bond was formed between Melissa and Jill.

During Ronnie Dunbar's trial for Melissa's murder, there was an effort to paint her as a young tearaway. Garda sources later said that she was very far from being wild. She may have become more difficult to control in the weeks leading up to her death, but she was described as being a quiet and timid girl. A senior garda told the *Sunday Tribune* after the trial that Melissa's problems had begun when she had started to hang around with the Dunbar girls. It was the Dunbar sisters who led the Mahon girls astray, not the other way around. The first time Melissa came into contact with gardaí was after she had been involved in a break-in at a house in Sligo with Samantha and Jill. Gardaí described the Dunbar girls as 'bold as brass' when they were caught redhanded, but that Melissa had been terrified. She understood that she had done something wrong.

Ultimately, Samantha and Melissa would become inseparable and through that friendship, Melissa would form a bond with Samantha and Jill's father, Ronnie Dunbar.

Ronnie Dunbar was born into a large Sligo family in September 1964. He moved to London in the mid-1980s where he married Angela Day and had a daughter, who they named Kirsty. He then met a 15-year-old girl named Lisa Conroy—she had been Kirsty's babysitter—and started a relationship with her. In the six or seven years they were together, she bore him three daughters. After Dunbar was sentenced in relation to Melissa's death, Lisa Conroy spoke to the *Gerry Ryan Show* and described her life with Dunbar:

When I first met the man I was young, 15 years old and I was in care. The relationship became sexual just before I was 16 years old. He was a big man. It was like he was my bodyguard. I was picked on and tormented a lot in the children's home and I just thought he was my knight in shining armour. He seemed very charming and reeled me in very well. I thought he was a nice person and I really liked him at the time.

Ronnie was very self-obsessed, always looking at himself in the mirror and putting on make-up. He did competitions in body building. I think all the steroids and smoking cannabis over the years has deluded his brain.

Ronnie likes to control everything, he's a control freak. He likes to manipulate people. He gets everything his own way all the time. He controlled me a lot. He made sure I had no friends. He felt very threatened when a great aunt of mine came on the scene because he knew I was coming into a lot of money because my dad passed away. He just really controlled me. I believed everything he said was right. He made sure I had no real contact with the outside world. I had three children from him at a very young age, all under the age of five, so he knew I'd be stuck in the house with the kids while he pranced around at the gym and got on with his life. He would demand sex from me and if I didn't give it to him he would just punch the living daylights out of me.

I said no to sex on a few occasions, but he did it anyway. When I was heavily pregnant with my first child, he bashed me over the sofa because I wouldn't give him sex. I was just very, very frightened of him. I couldn't stand up for myself. He kicked me in the stomach during my second pregnancy and I lost a twin—Samantha was a twin. It just went on and on and on. He's just a very aggressive man.

I had given birth to three girls by the time I was 20 and he was never there. I looked after the children most of the time. He was always in the gym. He was never really nasty to the girls from what I saw. He never showed any aggression towards the kids. It was just me at the time. They didn't really know him a lot because he was always out at the gym. He wasn't really there. He was having affairs. He walked out on me when I was carrying our youngest child. He came back to tell me he had moved out but he didn't tell me with whom. I found out it was a stripper. He said to me, 'Cry if you want to cry', but I didn't show him any tears. I had my little two and a half year old, Shirley, picking me up off the floor. She was saying, 'It's going to be all right, Mummy.' On another occasion, he kicked me in the leg and gave me a clot in my lung which I nearly died from. The violence towards me went on and on and, in the end, I just fled from it. I had no family, no one to talk to. I was totally vulnerable.

Shirley supported her mother's claims when, after the trial, she spoke to the *Sunday World* about her early life with Dunbar. Shirley said that there was violence in her home from as far back as she could remember. Her father beat her mother and she and her sisters were placed on the 'at risk' register as a result. She said her parents had even fought in front of their social workers. They had little money, although Dunbar wore the best clothes and spent all of his time at the gym. She did not remember him ever having a job. She said her mother had had to resort to shoplifting to clothe Shirley and her sisters.

Shirley remembered a night when she witnessed Dunbar trying to strangle her mother as she slept in bed, but Lisa woke up and the girls screamed at him until he stopped. She said, 'Another time, when I was five, I remember he kept punching her in the face and I could see the blood down her face and her nose.'

Eventually, Lisa decided that she could not take any further abuse and left Dunbar.

'When I ran away from Ronnie, I didn't take the children. I had nowhere to live and I was thinking, Oh my God, what a mistake. I went back for the children and he wouldn't give them to me. I went to the courts and signed a residence order which, really, kissed my kids goodbye, which I didn't realise would happen at the time.'

United Kingdom social services took the three girls away from Dunbar and placed them in foster care. A year later, however, they were returned to him.

In the summer of 2000, Dunbar became involved in a row with a London drug dealer who, according to Dunbar, sold crack cocaine. That fight led to a gun attack at his home in which he, and the then nine-year-old Shirley, were shot. By Dunbar's account, he had had a fist fight with the drug dealer in his gym after Dunbar had encouraged a number of young people to stop selling drugs for the man. Dunbar claimed to be anti-drugs but, according to his daughter and former wife, he constantly smoked cannabis and took performance enhancing steroids. He also has a criminal conviction in the United Kingdom for possession of a controlled substance.

Shirley told the *Sunday World*:

> A knock came to the door. This man was there with four of his friends and there was a confrontation at the door. I came out and was standing in the doorway between the hall and the kitchen. My dad slammed the door and then there was a bang. I felt a pain in my leg but I didn't equate the pain and the bang. I looked down and saw that the white trousers I was wearing were full of blood. I had been shot in the right thigh. I started crying with panic and pain. I heard him scream, 'You've shot my daughter. You've shot my daughter.' Dad ran. He was shot once in the back. He tells people that he was shot up to six times but this is not true. He shows people marks on his upper body which he says are bullet wounds. They are scars he got as a result of some sort of skin or blood disease he had years ago.

Dunbar agreed to give evidence against his assailant who was jailed following a trial. Dunbar and the girls were immediately placed in the witness protection programme and their surname was changed to McManus, which was Dunbar's mother's maiden name.

For the next five years, the family was moved to a number of locations in England before ending up in Scotland. Dunbar later told the *Sligo Weekender* that he returned to Ireland having suffered racist abuse in Scotland. In reality, he had been thrown out of the witness protection programme. When his removal from the programme came to light, he said it was because he had campaigned for better conditions for protected witnesses. He told a girlfriend, Angelique Sheridan, that he had been threatened in

Scotland but Shirley told the *Sunday World*, that the move to Ireland was because her father could not stop fighting with the locals in the village in which they had been placed.

Lisa said, 'How can you get your child shot and retain custody? They just seemed to stick by him and this shooting by this drug person seemed to do him a favour. When I tell my story, people don't believe me. How they can give the children to this man, but they did. It has ripped my world apart. Irish police contacted me after Melissa's death. They told me he had been arrested and interviewed. The next day, I was told he had been charged with her murder. He hasn't apologised to me. He only thinks of himself all the time. It's just about him. He hasn't got any thought for anybody as long as he can manipulate people to get what he wants.'

Dunbar's drug conviction in the UK was not his only run-in with the law over the years. At his sentence hearing at the Central Criminal Court in July 2009, Mr Justice Barry White heard that Dunbar had a number of previous convictions. His first court appearance was in November 1981 at Sligo District Court when he was bound to the peace for three months for criminal damage, burglary and larceny. In March of that year, he was convicted of two counts of assault and one count of robbery with violence. He received a 12-month suspended sentence. In July 1982, he was convicted of car theft and was sentenced to three months detention which, until July 2009, was his only custodial sentence. In England, he was sentenced in August 1995 for theft and shoplifting and received six months probation. In March 1995, he received a 12-month suspended sentence for the drugs conviction and, on 19 November 2007, at Sligo District Court, he was fined €100 for threatening abusive and insulting behaviour contrary to the Public Order Act.

Despite evidence to the contrary, Dunbar claimed he was an exemplary father who loved and cared deeply for his daughters. In 2005, when a troubled young girl began to visit his Sligo home regularly, he took her under his wing. In his account, he sought only to protect Melissa Mahon and act as a father figure to her.

Melissa's own parents, Mary and Frederick Mahon, were also

originally from Sligo. They had met in their home town and moved to England in 1969. There, they married and had ten children. Leeanna, their ninth child, was born on 15 March 1990 and, two years later, Melissa, their youngest, was born in Walthamstow on 10 March 1992.

The Mahon family regularly returned to Sligo for visits and even came back to live in the town for three or four years in the 1980s. On 12 July 2005, Mary travelled to Sligo because her father had passed away. She then stayed on to celebrate her upcoming birthday with her brothers and sisters. She decided to stay for good and sent word to her husband and younger children to join her. Mary later told the press that she felt that Sligo was a safer and better environment for her young daughters to grow up in, compared with London. She said she was concerned about the girls' personal safety and was worried about all of her children in the light of the growing threat of terrorist attacks in the United Kingdom.

The Central Criminal Court heard that while still living in England, the family had come to the attention of social services. Two of Melissa's older siblings were placed on the child protection register and three children had, on occasion, been taken into foster care—although, for one, it was only an overnight stay.

In late August 2005, Frederick, Leeanna and Melissa Mahon arrived in Sligo. Another sister, Yvonne, who was five years Melissa's senior, later joined the family and they moved into number 78 Rathbraughan Park, the same estate that Ronnie Dunbar lived in with his daughters.

Leeanna and Melissa Mahon started school in September and Melissa found herself in the same class as Jill Dunbar. In time, Jill, Melissa, Samantha and Leeanna became firm friends and the Mahon girls began to spend a large portion of their time at the Dunbar house. Mary Mahon knew Ronnie Dunbar to see and the Dunbar girls visited the Mahon house on one or two occasions that year. Largely, however, they spent all of their time, school nights and weekends, in the Dunbar house. He took them swimming and for drives in his small, blue Fiat Cinquecento.

They visited Sligo beaches and beauty spots such as Strandhill, Rossess Point and Slish Wood.

Leeanna noticed that Melissa and Ronnie were growing close to one another. He was heavily tattooed and, on one occasion, asked Melissa to rub Vaseline onto a new marking on his arm. Melissa and Dunbar sat side by side on the sofa as she tended to him. According to Leeanna, they were always sitting on the sofa together. On another occasion, Leeanna saw Melissa lying on the sofa with Ronnie, a middle-aged man. She was positioned between his legs with her head on his chest.

During Dunbar's trial, Leeanna was cross-examined at the Central Criminal Court by Dunbar's defence barrister, she agreed that she did not at the time think that there had been anything sinister going on between Ronnie and Melissa. Leeanna also accepted that Dunbar had barred Melissa from the house for a period during the school year because Melissa had been doing 'silly things'. Dunbar told Melissa not to return to the house until she had learned how to behave.

Another young girl who lived in the Rathbraughan Estate and attended Mercy College was 16 years old when she testified at Dunbar's trial. She was in the same class as Melissa but said that Melissa was often absent. When Melissa did show up, she would take a half day. The girl did not pal around with Melissa but would talk to her when they met. She also knew the Dunbar sisters who lived across the street from her. She got to know Ronnie Dunbar through his daughters and, as so many other young girls seemed to, she got along well with him. He would sometimes give her a lift in his blue Fiat, usually his daughters were in the car too. The girl said that they had sometimes taken spins out to Lough Gill, taking a route past Parkes Castle to a spot beside the River Bonet where a boat was tied to a tree.

The girl said that she had never been in the car at the same time as Melissa but had, once or twice, seen Melissa in Dunbar's car. On one occasion, she had spotted Melissa climbing into the boot of the vehicle. There were footballs in the boot and Melissa got in beside them. She fitted in easily.

The witness often saw Melissa in the Dunbar house. She said

Ronnie always sat on the sofa and Melissa would sit with him, leaning up against him. Samantha and Jill sat in armchairs.

As the school year continued, Leeanna visited the Dunbar house less and less until she eventually stopped going altogether, but as Leeanna's interest in the Dunbars waned, Melissa's attachment to her new friends grew. By the time summer 2006 rolled around, Melissa was spending most of her time in 64 Rathbraughan Park.

Mary and Frederick's eldest son, Anthony Mahon, lived in England with his wife and child and decided to visit his parents in July 2006. He stayed for two weeks and, during that time, Melissa slept on a blow-up bed in her mother's room. Yvonne took the sofa and Leeanna was in the box room. The day Anthony and his family were due to leave, Mary woke early to find that Melissa was missing from the house. She instinctively knew where her youngest child had disappeared to. She got Leeanna out of bed and marched down to number 64.

Mary banged on Ronnie Dunbar's door and it was opened, but quickly closed again, by Samantha. Mary and Leeanna waited several minutes until Dunbar appeared. Mary asked him if Melissa was in his house but he replied that she was not. He said he was only out of bed himself. Leeanna waited at the front door as Mary went into the house to look for her daughter. Mary went into the kitchen as Dunbar went out to his back garden to check the shed. Mary watched from the back door as he opened the shed to find Melissa, dressed in her night clothes, giggling with Samantha. The girls were ordered out of their hiding place. Mary was furious and gave Melissa a slap as she reached the kitchen before she brought her home.

Anthony Mahon and his family left Sligo that day and the sleeping arrangements in the Mahon house returned to normal with Yvonne and Melissa sharing the back bedroom. When Mary retired that evening, Melissa was dressed for bed but was awake and playing on a computer. Mary rose the following morning, 4 August, and, again, discovered that Melissa was gone. Melissa had left the sitting room window open in the course of her escape.

Mary waited until that evening to telephone Sligo Garda

Station to report that the now 14 year old was missing. She intimated that she was not too concerned as she believed the girl was in a neighbour's house and would return in her own good time. A week later, Mary called to Dunbar's house for the second and last time to ask Ronnie if he knew where her daughter was. He denied that she was in his house and said he would keep an eye out for her.

Mary would later tell the Central Criminal Court that she saw her daughter on two further occasions that summer. On the first, Mary was walking into town with Leeanna and Yvonne when they saw Melissa sitting on a garden shed in the Rathbraughan Estate. She had dyed her hair jet black and it was shorter than usual. Days later, Melissa called to the Mahon house to shower and change her clothes. She stayed for dinner and then a social worker from the Health Service Executive arrived to pick her up and return her to the residential care unit she had been placed in. That was the last time Mary saw her daughter.

The court heard that Melissa had made allegations that she had been physically abused by her mother and sexually abused by her father. She did not, however, make any statement to gardaí to that effect. Mary agreed in court that she was informed at the time that Melissa had made the accusations. Mary also accepted that when Melissa was reported missing for the last time on 14 September 2006, she had refused to make a statement to gardaí about her daughter. Gardaí repeatedly asked her to co-operate but she declined. She told the court, 'It wasn't up to me. She wasn't in my care.'

Mary had been unhappy about the allegations Melissa had made and, as far as she was concerned, her daughter no longer had a family.

03 | CARE

Catherine Farrelly was a social worker and had been employed by the Health Service Executive since November 2004. She was based in Markievicz House in Sligo as a member of the Children and Family Social Worker Team. She came to know the Mahon family in March 2006, when, as she told the Central Criminal Court, she had been referred to the family in relation to a matter which was unconnected to the trial of Ronnie Dunbar.

As she got to know the family, it became apparent to Catherine that Melissa was having difficulty with her attendance at Mercy College. Melissa was unhappy at the school and, in May of that year, a discussion took place between Melissa, her mother, Catherine Farrelly and the school's head teacher about how best to deal with her difficulties. Melissa expressed an interest in moving to St Joseph's, a school in Sligo for students aged five to 18 with special needs who have been assessed as having mild, general learning disabilities. Melissa was assessed but was deemed to be of average intelligence and not, therefore, someone who required the services of the school.

Catherine met Melissa in June and July 2006 and it was decided that a further discussion would be held between her and the Mahon family over the summer break to determine how

Melissa's poor attendance could be improved. On 10 August, Catherine contacted the Mahon family to arrange a home visit but was put off by Mary Mahon until 22 August. When Catherine arrived at the Mahon home, she found out that Melissa had been missing from the house since 4 August.

Garda Daniel Cummins was on duty at Sligo Garda Station in the radio control room on the morning of 4 August when Mary Mahon called to say that Melissa had gone missing. Mary told him that Melissa was in a neighbour's house and would come back when she was ready, she described Melissa as being of slight build, having an English accent and wearing a pink top.

When Catherine Farrelly discovered the truth of Melissa's situation on 22 August, she immediately contacted the gardaí and brought Mary Mahon down to Sligo Garda Station.

Garda Pat Conway was on duty that evening and, at 6.10 p.m., was told that two ladies wanted to speak to him in private. He met with Mary and Catherine and they told him that Melissa had been missing since earlier in the month. Mary said she had telephoned the station on 4 August to report her daughter as missing. She told Garda Conway that she believed that her daughter was probably in Ronnie Dunbar's house.

Mary was sent home, but Catherine and Garda Conway teamed up and decided to pay Ronnie Dunbar a visit. Garda Conway had known Dunbar for years and felt he had a relationship with him.

It was the first time that Catherine met Dunbar and she spoke to him in the presence of his daughter, Samantha, at the front of his house. Dunbar told Catherine that he did not know where Melissa was. His story was that he had received a call from the girl from a phonebox in Tesco's car park on 4 August but had not seen or heard from her since. He said he was very concerned for her but had absolutely no idea where she could be. He admitted that Melissa had spent a fair amount of time with his daughters that summer and had been in his house on 3 August but he said she had been annoyed with him. He then told Catherine that if Melissa had been missing for over two weeks, he could not understand why the authorities were not already looking for her.

He believed she had left her own home for a very specific reason and alluded to her being the victim of sexual abuse. He told Garda Conway that he thought his daughter Shirley might have spotted Melissa at an amusement arcade. He also suggested that they should talk to Melissa's sister Leeanna. Garda Conway noted that Dunbar was talking more to Catherine than to him, despite the fact that he already knew Dunbar and that Catherine had only just met him. He suspected that Dunbar was hiding something.

The social worker felt that Melissa was likely to either be in Dunbar's house or at a location of which he was fully aware. Catherine and Garda Conway left his house and visited Shirley Dunbar who lived apart from her family to see if she had any information, but she didn't.

The pair returned to Dunbar's house at 9 p.m. but he continued to state that he did not know where Melissa was and said that he was as worried about her as they were. He remarked that he was well respected within certain groups in the community and would try to put the word out that he was looking for information about the missing girl. Dunbar said he had three daughters himself and knew it was not easy to deal with teenage girls. He also mentioned he was in a happy relationship with a woman at the time.

'I hope you don't think she's in the house,' he told Garda Conway. 'If you wish, you're free to search it.'

Garda Conway declined to conduct a search. He later told the Central Criminal Court that he knew Dunbar 'of old' and at that stage he 'feared the worst'. Dunbar told him that he would put feelers out among the Travelling community and would contact Garda Conway if he heard anything useful.

The following morning, 23 August, Dunbar showed up at Markievicz House looking for Catherine Farrelly. He told her that he had managed to contact Melissa and she had agreed to phone her later that day. Catherine gave him the social work team mobile number to pass on to Melissa. At 4 p.m. the same day, Melissa rang Catherine who managed to convince the teenager to come to meet her at Markievicz House. Melissa said she would be in touch later to make the arrangements.

Catherine kept the Mahon family informed of the development and then went again to the Dunbar house in the company of Garda Conway. Dunbar met them at the gate. He said he was surprised that Melissa had agreed to a meeting but said he would do his best to encourage her to follow through with it, though he also said he couldn't promise anything. He still claimed not to know where Melissa was and said that he had his own daughters to look after, though he hoped that Melissa would contact him again. He said she was 'a very hurt and a very frightened human being'.

At this stage, Garda Conway and Catherine Farrelly believed that Dunbar was their only link to the girl.

The next day, 24 August, Dunbar telephoned Catherine and told her that Melissa had been in touch with him and had agreed to a meeting but had laid down four conditions. He warned Catherine that the stipulations had to be met or Melissa would disappear. Firstly, gardaí were not to be made aware that a meeting was taking place and they certainly should not be present at it. Secondly, Dunbar and Samantha had to be there. Thirdly, Catherine had to travel to the meeting, which was to be held at an as yet undisclosed location, in Dunbar's car. Finally, Melissa would contact Dunbar to tell him where the location of the meeting would be.

These were unusual requests and Catherine consulted her superiors before she agreed to go ahead. It was decided that as Melissa was a missing person and the authorities needed to know that she was alive, Catherine should agree to the plan. Catherine told Dunbar that she was not happy about the mode of transport and wanted to travel in her own car but he told her that Melissa's demands were unequivocal and she would not talk to Catherine if she saw a vehicle other than Dunbar's.

Later that day, at 2 p.m., Dunbar rang Catherine and told her to meet him outside Markievicz House. He arrived, with Samantha, to take her to the meeting in his little blue car. At around 2.15 p.m., Melissa rang Dunbar's mobile and, after the call, he started driving. They drove for nearly half an hour along a circuitous route until they ended up at a clearing in Slish Wood.

Catherine felt as though they had been driving backwards and forwards in the least direct route possible in an effort to confuse her and disguise the location of the meeting place. Catherine saw Melissa sitting alone at a picnic table as Dunbar turned his car into the clearing. Her appearance had changed. She was well dressed but her hair was darker than Catherine remembered. Samantha ran to her friend and threw her arms around her as if they had not met for a long time. Dunbar also behaved as if he had not seen Melissa for weeks.

When Catherine sat down to talk to Melissa, Samantha placed herself beside the girl but Dunbar only stayed at the table for a short time and then walked off into the woods. Catherine did not need to ask him to leave them alone. She spent around 20 minutes trying to persuade Melissa to go into a Health Service Executive residential care centre at Lis na nÓg. During their conversation, Melissa alleged that she had been sexually abused by her father and had suffered violence at the hands of her mother. Samantha told Catherine that she had seen marks on Melissa's back where she had been burned with cigarettes. Melissa agreed. She told Catherine that she was not prepared to go back to her own home but neither did she want go into care. Catherine explained that, no matter how much Melissa might want to live with the Dunbars, it was simply not an option.

Dunbar returned from his wander and supported Catherine's argument. He told Melissa that going into care was for the best. Melissa was unconvinced. She wanted to be fostered by Dunbar and his then girlfriend, Angelique Sheridan, or by the people she said she had been staying with, although she did not say who those people were.

Dunbar referred to the incident on 3 August when Melissa had been slapped by her mother after she had been found hiding in his shed. Melissa told Catherine that she had wet herself when her mother had hit her. Catherine tried to explain to Melissa that she needed to be somewhere safe, but Melissa was adamant that she would not go into care.

She then told Catherine that their time was up and she had to leave. Dunbar and Catherine both expressed concern about leaving her alone in the woods but she refused to go with them. She said she would contact Dunbar in half an hour to let him know that she was safe. Catherine reluctantly got back into the car and left Melissa in the woods.

Dunbar drove Catherine back to Markievicz House but, by the time they arrived, they had still not heard word from Melissa. Catherine left Dunbar and contacted Garda Conway. She also rang the Mahon family to tell them about he meeting and later rang Dunbar twice to see if Melissa had been in touch. At 7 p.m., Dunbar told Catherine that he had spoken to Melissa and that they had made an arrangement to talk again the following day.

On 25 August, Catherine and Garda Conway met with a superior within the Health Service Executive to discuss Melissa's case. They agreed to remain in contact with Dunbar and bring him on board with the purpose of getting Melissa into the care of the Health Service Executive. They rang him ask him to come to Markievicz House to discuss how to proceed. He arrived there, with Samantha, and told Garda Conway and Catherine that he would stay in touch with Melissa and would do his best to encourage her to go into care. Later the same day, at around 5 p.m., he telephoned Catherine and said he had good news.

During that conversation, Catherine found Dunbar difficult to follow but believed that the gist of what he was saying was that Melissa was now willing to go into care. Catherine asked if she could come to his house and talk to him face to face but he refused saying that he was a busy man and it just was not possible. He told Catherine that he would see her the next day.

The following day was a Saturday, and Catherine and Garda Conway met at Sligo Garda Station and telephoned Dunbar. He said he was busy but agreed to meet them outside the gym he went to. They met him in the car park and Dunbar got into the back of Garda Conway's own car and repeated that he was a busy man and that this business was having an effect on his life. He told them that he was hopeful that Melissa would agree to go into care but she would not do so until Monday and would contact Catherine over the weekend to make the necessary arrangements. On Sunday evening, Garda Conway went alone to Dunbar's house. Dunbar told him that he had not heard from Melissa and again invited Garda Conway to search the house. Again, Garda Conway declined.

Monday, 28 August arrived and Catherine had heard nothing from Melissa and so, again, rang Dunbar. He said Melissa was still willing to go into care and would do so later that day. At this stage, Catherine and her team leader decided to go to Sligo District Court and apply for an Emergency Care Order under the 1991 Child Care Act.

The purpose of the Child Care Act is to promote the safety and welfare of children by giving powers to the Health Service Executive, then known as the Health Board, to take such steps as it considers necessary to identify children who are not receiving adequate care and protection.

Section 12 of the act deals with children deemed to be in emergency situations. It was an order under that section that the social workers wanted to seek. This section states that where a garda has reasonable grounds for believing that there is an immediate and serious risk to the health or welfare of a child and it would not be sufficient for the protection of the child to wait for an application to be made by the Health Board under section 13 of the act, the garda may enter any building and remove the child to safety. The garda may use force if necessary. The garda then must deliver the child to the custody of the Health Board which must apply within three days to the District Court for an Emergency Care Order under section 13 of the act which allows the Health Board to retain custody of the child for a further eight days, if the judge is satisfied that the child is in danger. The Health Board is also obligated to keep the parents of any such child informed of developments.

However, before the application was made, Dunbar arranged for Melissa to go to the residential unit, Lis na nÓg. Melissa arrived at the care home with Dunbar and Samantha at 4 p.m on 28 August. The house rules were explained to Melissa in the presence of Samantha. Lis na nÓg housed children between the ages of 12 and 18 of either gender for a maximum of six months after the child has been taken into the care of the Health Service

Executive. It was a small four-bedroom house. Two staff would be on duty at all times. Residents were able walk in and out of the house. There was no lock in and the success of the unit depended very much upon the co-operation of its residents.

Social workers agreed to drive Melissa to Dunbar's house at 8 p.m. as long as he returned her to the home by 10 p.m. Staff checked Melissa's room at 10.30 p.m. and she had returned as arranged. She had been very upset about going into the unit but seemed to be fine that night. Catherine continued to check on Melissa in the following days.

On 30 August, Catherine arrived at Lis na nÓg in the afternoon to speak to Melissa but she had already left with Samantha and Dunbar earlier in the day. Catherine rang Melissa's mobile and arranged to meet her at Lis na nÓg at 4 p.m. Melissa did not show up. Catherine then went to Dunbar's house and spent three hours there with Melissa and a number of other young people, including Samantha, Jill and a younger girl from across the street. Catherine learned that Dunbar was due to go into hospital to receive treatment for a boil. Melissa was reluctant to go back to Lis na nÓg and Catherine tried in vain to convince her to co-operate. Melissa was upset that Dunbar was going into hospital. She told Catherine that he was her father now and she would not leave him. Catherine looked to Dunbar to back her up, but he appeared to be ambivalent about the situation. While he encouraged Melissa to return to the home, he did not want to push her too far and risk alienating her. At 7 p.m., Melissa ran out of the Dunbar house and Samantha said she was heading to the Mahon house. Catherine got the impression that Dunbar was very worried and annoyed that she would go to back to her own parents. Catherine rang Melissa's mobile and telephoned the Mahon house but got no response and so waited outside Lis na nÓg hoping that Melissa would eventually return to the unit.

At 8 p.m., Melissa had still not shown up at the care home but Dunbar phoned the social work team mobile to tell Catherine that Melissa was with him. He agreed to bring her back to Lis na nÓg but said that Melissa had refused to get into his car. She was still unhappy about him going into hospital and said she wanted to stay with him. Eventually, she acquiesced when Samantha got into the car with her. Dunbar took the girls for food and, an hour later, brought Melissa back to the home.

Melissa visited Dunbar at the hospital the following morning but went back to Lis na nÓg in the afternoon to talk to Catherine. She said she was afraid to go back to school and did not feel safe there. They discussed the possibility of Melissa receiving home tuition but Catherine explained that Melissa would have to start spending more time in Lis na nÓg to enable the staff to engage with her properly in a therapeutic way. She told Melissa that it was important that she gave herself a real chance to settle in and deal with the issues that had been troubling her. Essentially, she needed to spend less time with Ronnie Dunbar.

Dunbar was still in hospital on Friday, 1 September and Melissa visited him again. Catherine received a phone call from the manager of Lis na nÓg to say that when staff went to the hospital to collect Melissa at 8 p.m., she was not there. They had tried to contact her on her mobile but she had not answered, so they had gone to Dunbar's house. Samantha had answered the door but had said that Melissa was not there and that she did not know where she was. Melissa remained missing for the rest of that night. She returned to Lis na nÓg in the early hours of Saturday morning but left again soon afterwards.

That Saturday afternoon, Garda Adrian Dockery and Garda Aisling Fallon were on patrol in a garda vehicle when they received a call that Melissa was missing from Lis na nÓg. Garda Dockery would come to know Melissa well during the course of her stay at the care centre. Locating Melissa became a recurring part of his patrol duties.

A second call came through that afternoon from a male who reported that Melissa was in the area of Half Moon Bay in Hazelwood. The man said she had run into the woods and was sniffing gas. The gardaí drove to the car park at that location and found Dunbar sitting in his car—he had made the call. He said he had been discharged from hospital and had driven Melissa and Samantha to the woods but they had run off into the forest and were refusing to come out. He, again, claimed that they were sniffing gas.

Dunbar did not want to follow the girls because of his recent hospitalisation. He was stressed and wanted the gardaí to find the girls and bring them back to him as quickly as possible. Garda Dockery ventured into the woods. He could hear girls giggling and laughing and then spotted Melissa and Samantha. They tried to run away from him but he caught them easily. Melissa's clothes were damp and soiled from being in the woods and she insisted that she be allowed to go back to Dunbar's house to wash and change. Dunbar was angry with the girls but offered to take them home and then bring Melissa back to Lis na nÓg. Garda Dockery agreed to the arrangement and informed the care home of the plan but, later that evening, he received a call from Lis na nÓg informing him that Melissa had not been returned as promised.

Melissa made an appearance at the unit on Sunday, 3 September, but went missing again until Monday. This time Dunbar rang Lis na nÓg to report that he had contacted Melissa and would bring her back.

Garda Pat Conway was often made aware of Melissa's disappearances from the residential care unit. On the last day of August, he was on patrol when he found Melissa and Samantha walking away from Lis na nÓg. Melissa had told him that she would return, but, when he called to the unit later, he was told that she had not kept her word. On 1 September, he received a call from a friend who told him that Melissa was drinking in a field with other young people. Between 1 and 13 September, Garda Conway rang Melissa on a number of occasions advising her to return to Lis na nÓg. He also called to the Dunbar house regularly to see if she was there and Ronnie Dunbar would invariably tell him that she was not in the house and then advise him to go and ask the Mahons where their daughter was.

Catherine went to Lis na nÓg when she heard that Melissa had returned on Monday, 4 September. She found Melissa in her bedroom with Samantha but Melissa refused to speak to her. She was angry with Catherine and accused her of trying to get her out of Dunbar's house the previous Wednesday.

The following day, a staff meeting was held by social workers in Melissa's absence to determine the best course of action. Staff decided to invite Dunbar to attend a placement-planning meeting in Lis na nÓg on Wednesday, 6 September. He had to be told that Melissa was not settling in and that the time she was spending in his house was not helping the situation. The purpose of the meeting was to discuss the possibility of reducing his level of contact with Melissa. Catherine continued to keep the Mahon family informed of what was going on and visited their home that evening. They did not attend the placement-planning meeting.

The Central Criminal Court heard from Catherine that Mary Mahon was very negative about the prospect of Melissa rejoining her family. Mary was unhappy about the allegations that had been made by her daughter and felt that her husband had suffered enough. Catherine told the court that the UK social services were aware of a history of similar accusations from other family members. Nothing had been proved and the last accusation had been made in 1992, the year Melissa was born. Mary Mahon told Catherine Farrelly that, because of the allegations Melissa had made, either she or another family member would beat Melissa up if they saw her. This attitude combined with Melissa's accusations led her social workers to decide Melissa should not have contact with her family.

Donna McTague was the acting social care manager at Lis na nÓg during the time Melissa was a resident. She was aware of Melissa's reluctance to stay in the house and initially facilitated contact with the Dunbar family. She arranged pick-ups with Dunbar and received calls from him when Melissa showed up at his house. At first, she thought he was very helpful and she organised for Melissa to visit him while he was in hospital.

She was on duty at Lis na nÓg on 6 September, the day of the planned meeting in which staff hoped to persuade Dunbar that the current situation was untenable. Melissa left the home without permission at 11 a.m. but Dunbar telephoned the home to tell staff that she was at his house and that he would bring her back in the afternoon.

As Catherine Farrelly approached the care home for the meeting, she saw Dunbar outside with Samantha and Melissa. He was shouting at a teenage boy who was a resident of the home. Donna McTague heard Dunbar chastising the boy for spending the night in his house and in his bed with a girlfriend when he had been in hospital. Dunbar was aggressive and verbally abusive towards the boy and also accused him of smoking cannabis at the back of Lis na nÓg. Dunbar ordered Samantha to look for the remains of joints that had been smoked. He then turned to Melissa to seek her agreement with his accusations but she seemed distinctly uncomfortable and only nodded very slightly. Dunbar was told that it would be the Lis na nÓg staff, rather than him, who would deal with any incidents that happened in the home.

The social workers went inside for the meeting and asked Dunbar to wait in the kitchen while staff spoke to Melissa. Donna explained to him that they would bring him into the latter part of the meeting. He stayed for a number of minutes but soon became annoyed. Donna was making her way to him to ask him to join them when he decided to leave. He told her the Health Service Executive was unable to look after young people. He accused her of not supporting him in his earlier attack on the teenage boy. Donna pointed out that Dunbar was an adult and had been attacking a vulnerable teenage boy. She said it had not been appropriate to speak to the boy in that manner. Dunbar then alleged that it was Melissa that the boy had been in bed with. Melissa had followed Donna out of the meeting and was tearfully listening to this exchange. Dunbar asked the girl if what he had said was correct. She nodded. He left the unit and Melissa followed him. Donna sensed that Melissa was fearful—her hands were shaking and she was close to tears. Donna asked her to stay but, as usual, she left with Dunbar and Samantha.

On one of the afternoons during this period, Fiona Keogh, another member of the staff at the home, was making Melissa's bed. Fiona had met Dunbar only once when he called to the unit with Samantha to collect Melissa. While making the bed, she found a photograph of Dunbar under Melissa's pillow. It was a circular cut out of his face from a larger standard-sized photograph. On the back was written: 'Best Wishes, McManus'. Fiona placed the picture on Melissa's bedside locker and told Donna McTague about what she had found.

On 7 September, Catherine discovered that Melissa had again not slept at Lis na nÓg. This was the final straw. She and Donna McTague went to Sligo District Court to apply for an order under section 47 of the Child Care Act, which provides that where a child is in the care of the Health Service Executive, the court may give directions or make an order about any issue affecting the welfare of the child as it thinks proper.

The social workers successfully applied to the court for an order that Ronnie Dunbar should not be allowed to have contact with Melissa Mahon without the prior consent of the Health Service Executive. Garda Conway telephoned Dunbar that morning to request his presence at the hearing. Dunbar initially agreed to attend but later changed his mind. He was annoyed that gardaí had come to his house looking for Melissa who was, again, missing from the care home. That afternoon, a one-month care order and a direction under section 47 were granted by Judge Oliver McGuinness at Sligo District Court.

Catherine and a colleague, Ria Openhaufen, had visited Dunbar at his house on their way to the courthouse. They told him that their concerns for Melissa had increased. She was not spending an adequate amount of time in the care unit and his involvement with her was, in their opinion, preventing her from settling in properly. He was annoyed by the fact that they were going to seek a court order and told them they were stitching him up. They had initially sought his help with Melissa and now they wanted him to stay away from her.

Dunbar was informed when the order was granted and its terms were clearly explained to him. That evening, Catherine met Melissa and told her about the new state of affairs. She told the girl that it was not the case that she could never see Dunbar again. The order meant that their access to each other would be restricted to give her time to settle into Lis na nÓg properly. Melissa was upset and reacted tearfully to the news. Dunbar telephoned the unit that evening in a conciliatory mood. He wanted to smooth over matters regarding his disagreement with the teenage boy at Lis na nÓg. Dunbar told Catherine that he was aware that she and the Health Service Executive had Melissa's best interests at heart. Catherine told him that his compliance with the court order would demonstrate that he, too, was only concerned with Melissa's best interests.

In the wake of the court order, Melissa's behaviour deteriorated. She spent an increasing amount of time with other young people and was experimenting with sniffing gas and drinking alcohol.

By Monday, 11 September, Melissa had been missing from the care home for most of the weekend. She had shown up on the Sunday but had left again and made a brief appearance on Monday. It was thought that she had spent the night in an empty house with another young person. On Tuesday, Catherine saw Melissa at Markievicz House where she tried to convince her to return to Lis na nÓg but Melissa refused and spent another night missing.

Garda Conway went to the Dunbar house that evening but was told that Melissa had not been seen. In the early hours of 12 September, Dunbar telephoned Lis na nÓg and told staff that Melissa was in the Caltragh Estate on the outskirts of Sligo. That evening, she was found by gardaí in bed in a house with another girl and three young men. She was returned to the unit but was in defiant form, disrespectful and agitated. She left the house at 4 a.m. and was found in the centre of town by gardaí. She threatened to cut her wrists if she was not brought back to the Caltragh Estate to collect something. Only then would she agree to go back to Lis na nÓg.

By 13 September, foster care was being suggested by Melissa's social workers as they considered her to be at increasing risk. There had been intense police involvement with the teenager for the previous two weeks, with gardaí having been called on an almost daily basis. Her behaviour had been poor from the beginning but the situation had worsened considerably as time had gone on.

On 13 September, Garda Dockery was informed that Melissa was, again, missing and that she might be found in, again, Caltragh. He arrived at 3.20 p.m. and saw a number of youths hanging around a green area of the estate. He recognised Melissa who was with another teenage girl who was also a Lis na nÓg resident. The girls ran in opposite directions when they spotted the patrol car but were soon caught. Both had superficial, self-inflicted cuts along their forearms and had broken glass and a razor blade in their pockets.

The girls struggled but were, nevertheless, brought back to Lis na nÓg. Staff asked the gardaí to stay for a while in case the girls needed to be kept under control. Melissa immediately barricaded herself into a bathroom and tried to smash the window to get out. With the permission of staff, who were concerned for her safety, Garda Dockery forced open the door.

Of the 16 nights that Melissa was officially resident in Lis na nÓg, she was missing for eight. She always left without permission. There were 11 notifications of her being reported missing on the garda PULSE computer system. The placement was not working out. She had been coming and going as she pleased. She regarded the Dunbars as her family and wanted to spend all of her time with them. Her behaviour was defiant and she could not be cajoled or encouraged into co-operating with her social workers.

Arrangements had been made for a temporary foster care placement and when she was extracted from the bathroom, it was decided that it was time for Melissa to go to the foster family. She refused to travel in Catherine's car and had to be driven by gardaí to a house in Kinlough, County Leitrim. Melissa blamed Catherine for taking her away from the only person who had ever loved her. In the patrol car on the way to the foster home, she calmed down but was still upset that she was being taken away from Sligo. As she approached her new home, she became less agitated and increasingly resigned to her fate.

Jane McCall had been fostering children for several years in her large and welcoming home in Kinlough. She was well known to social workers and sprang to Catherine's mind when it was decided that someone needed to take Melissa in on a temporary basis. Jane was happy to help the girl and Melissa arrived with Catherine and the gardaí that evening in time for dinner. Catherine had bought Melissa mobile phone credit on the way to Kinlough to enable her to telephone an adult sister in England. She had also bought her cigarettes. As Catherine introduced Melissa to her foster carer, it was clear that the girl was withdrawn and upset. She gradually began to relax and Catherine and the gardaí left her to settle in. As Jane showed Melissa around the house, she warned her to be careful on the stairs leading to her bedroom, to which Melissa replied, 'Don't worry, I'll be running up and down them in no time at all.'

Melissa ate dinner and watched some television. She asked Jane if her friends could visit and was told that, of course, they could, when she had had a proper chance to settle in. After 11 p.m., Melissa changed for bed and negotiated the staircase to her room. Jane McCall was satisfied that Melissa was comfortable in her home and had seemed settled and happy when she had gone to bed. Jane had noticed recent slash marks on the girl's wrists but remarked to her husband how charming, polite and pretty Melissa was.

However, near midnight, the situation changed dramatically. Jane heard Melissa's mobile phone ring and then saw her come out of her room and go outside in her night clothes. She had a packet of cigarettes in her hand and was in floods of tears. Jane tried to coax her back into the house but Melissa wanted to be driven to Sligo immediately. Jane grabbed hold of her wrist but Melissa screamed at her, 'I'll have you for assault if you touch me.'

She had to let her go. Catherine Farrelly had instructed her to let Melissa run if she tried to leave. As hard as it was to do, Jane let go. As soon as she released Melissa's arm, the girl bolted up the lane in her bare feet. Jane rang the gardaí and the social worker and then jumped into her car to drive into Kinlough to look for Melissa.

Melissa had taken off into the night. It was dark and she didn't know where she was or how to do the one thing she had to do— get back to Sligo.

Hugh Fergus was at home with his wife, Rita, when he heard a knock at the door. It was well after midnight when he found a young girl with no shoes on looking up at him. She asked him to ring her father in Sligo and tell him where she was, then she handed over Ronnie Dunbar's number, explaining the different surname by saying that she had taken her mother's maiden name. She said she had fallen asleep under a tree and didn't know how she had got there. She was worried about a friend in Sligo who was pregnant.

Rita Fergus was suspicious—she knew that people who lived close by fostered children. As her husband rang the number he had been given, Rita rang gardaí at Manorhamilton. Melissa sat at the Fergus' kitchen table and waited for Ronnie Dunbar to rescue her.

Gardaí brought Catherine Farrelly to Hugh Fergus' house in the early hours of the morning. She found Melissa crying at the kitchen table and took her to Manorhamilton Garda Station where they spent the night. Melissa told Catherine that she had asked Mr Fergus to contact Dunbar. She was upset and thought he would be worried about her so Catherine allowed her to send him a text message from the social worker team mobile saying that she was okay and that she was with Catherine. Dunbar sent a text in reply saying, 'Thank God, I was worried.'

The following day, Catherine woke Melissa at 8 a.m. and they left the garda station. They stopped at a petrol station so Catherine could buy a breakfast roll for Melissa. Catherine left Melissa alone in the car and when she returned, she heard her on her mobile speaking to a male voice. According to an analysis of mobile phone records, Dunbar telephoned Melissa just before 8.15 a.m and the call lasted for eight minutes and five seconds.

Catherine then brought Melissa into Sligo town and they went to Dunnes Stores to buy her fresh clothes. They then stopped at Markievicz House to enable Melissa to change. Catherine had to work out what to do next with her charge, and so left her in the downstairs ladies toilet while she went to her office to make phone calls. It was after 10.30 a.m. and it was the last time Catherine saw Melissa Mahon. Phone records indicated that

Dunbar called Melissa's mobile just before 11 a.m. He would later —incorrectly—tell gardaí that the last contact he had with Melissa was the text message from the social worker team mobile saying that she was safe.

Ria Openhaufen, Catherine Farrelly's colleague at Markievicz House, saw Catherine arrive with Melissa at around 10 a.m. After Catherine realised that Melissa had run away again, it was Ria who telephoned Sligo Garda Station at around 12 noon to report her missing. Garda Katrina Hastings was on duty in the radio room and received Ria's call at 12.02 p.m. Ria said that Melissa had run out of Markievicz House at 10.30 a.m. No explanation was given for the delay between Melissa's departure and the phone call to gardaí.

An analysis of the phone traffic between Melissa and Dunbar for the months of July through to September was later carried out by gardaí. During Dunbar's trial the Central Criminal Court would hear that over 18 per cent of all the calls Dunbar made during the period were to Melissa. By comparison, just over 7 per cent were to his then girlfriend, Angelique Sheridan. Over 52 per cent of the text messages he sent were to Melissa, whereas only 21 per cent were to Angelique.

On the morning of her final disappearance, two text messages were sent from Melissa to Dunbar just before he called her as she sat alone in Catherine's car. Three further text messages were sent by Melissa to Dunbar between 9.45 a.m. and 10.45 a.m. that morning. Dunbar also called her before 11 a.m. and followed the call with a text message to her. She sent him another text at 10.50 a.m. and he called her at 10.52 a.m. By that time, she had left Markievicz House and was heading in the direction of the Rathbraughan Estate.

After Catherine realised that Melissa had left Markievicz House, she received a phone call from Lis na nÓg saying that Melissa had been sighted on the road leading to the Rathbraughan Estate.

Catherine Devaney had been a child-care key worker at Lis na nÓg for almost 15 years. That morning, she was driving a van past St John's Hospital towards Sligo town with Judith McLoughlin, the manager of Lis na nÓg, as her passenger. The women saw Melissa alone on the opposite side of the road walking towards the Rathbraughan Estate. Ms Devaney was surprised to see her as she had been on duty when Melissa had been transferred to the foster home the previous day. She had also been on duty when Garda Henry Rodgers had rung Lis na nÓg at 12.05 a.m. that morning to say that Melissa had telephoned Sligo Garda Station to say that she did not know where she was and could not find her way home. Catherine Devaney had also received a call from Ronnie Dunbar in the middle of the night to say he had been telephoned by a man in Kinlough who had said Melissa was in his house. Catherine Devaney had advised Dunbar to call Sligo Garda Station because Melissa was no longer officially in the care of Lis na nÓg.

Catherine Devaney stopped the van and Judith McLoughlin got out and called out Melissa's name. Melissa had been walking but when she saw the women, she started to run towards Rathbraughan. She was wearing a pink hooded top and dark tracksuit bottoms. The women did not go after her.

Catherine Devaney returned to Lis na nÓg and rang Catherine Farrelly at Markievicz House to report the sighting. She described Melissa to the Central Criminal Court as a small girl, very slightly built, fragile and unkempt. She said that the last time she saw Melissa, her once-brown hair was dyed a severe black. It had been dyed the night of the aborted placement meeting when Dunbar had left with Melissa before anyone had had an opportunity to talk to him.

Catherinie Devaney had also known Samantha from the time she spent with Melissa in Lis na nÓg. She said Samantha was very protective of Melissa but was not as respectful to staff as she should have been. Samantha was said to be a disruptive influence and tended to take over, not allowing Melissa to speak.

04 | MISSING

Sergeant Tom Colsh was on duty in a garda patrol car on 15 September, the day after Melissa was reported missing by the Health Service Executive staff. Social workers contacted the garda station to ask if there was any news about the teenager. Sergeant Ronan Mooney received a call from Catherine Farrelly asking if someone could check whether or not Melissa was in Ronnie Dunbar's house. He then directed Sergeant Colsh to go to 64 Rathbraughan Park to make enquires about the girl's whereabouts.

When Sergeant Colsh arrived at the house, it was empty. He turned to leave and a man appeared outside the neighbouring house. Sergeant Colsh asked him if he had seen the resident of number 64. The man introduced himself as Ronald McManus and said he had not seen anyone from that house in a long time. Another garda patrol car arrived and a garda who knew Ronnie Dunbar informed Sergeant Colsh that he had been speaking to the very man he was looking for.

Sergeant Colsh confronted Dunbar who then admitted he was the former resident of number 64 and had moved into the neighbouring house that week. He said he sometimes went by the name McManus. He said he had not heard from Melissa in a while and had not seen her since she had been last reported missing. He had been trying to help the Health Service Executive keep the girl on the straight and narrow. Sergeant Colsh then searched number 63 and found Dunbar's daughters in the house but there was no sign of Melissa.

Garda Pat Conway went to visit Dunbar four days later and also discovered that he had moved into the neighbouring house. He asked Dunbar to make contact with Melissa but Dunbar was reluctant to get involved. He did not appreciate the way he had been treated by the gardaí and the Health Service Executive. He was unhappy that his house had been searched and felt strongly that the finger of blame was being pointed at him. He said he would do his best but could not promise anything.

On 6 October, Garda Conway again visited Dunbar at his home who, again, insisted that he had not seen nor heard from Melissa. He invited Garda Conway in to search the house in the presence of Samantha, Shirley and Jill. Garda Conway conducted a search but there was no trace of Melissa. On this occasion, Dunbar was very co-operative. The house was searched again four days later but, by this stage, Dunbar's patience had begun to wear thin. As Garda Conway drove back to the station from the Rathbraughan Estate, Dunbar rang him to complain about the continued searches of his house.

Dunbar also telephoned Catherine Farrelly on 10 October, when he told her about the search and said he was extremely angry. He was also unhappy about the garda appeal for information about Melissa's whereabouts. He said the truth had not been told about the Health Service Executive's involvement in her disappearance and he threatened to go public with what he knew. Catherine warned him that such a course of action would not be in Melissa's best interest. His complaints about how the authorities had behaved in relation to Melissa were a common theme of his interaction with Catherine.

Catherine told the court that the Health Service Executive had been advised that it would be better not to mention in the media the fact that Melissa was in its care when she went missing.

Garda Conway, accompanied by Detective Inspector Colm Nevin, visited the Dunbar home again on 15 November 2006.

Dunbar reiterated that he had not seen Melissa since she had been in Lis na nÓg, saying he had not heard a word from her. He felt she was no longer in Sligo and said she could be anywhere. He repeated his complaints about the authorities and how he felt he had been badly treated.

During the trial, Garda Conway acknowledged a lack of cooperation from the Mahon family following Melissa's disappearance. He said, 'Mary felt that the Health Service Executive was responsible so she didn't make a statement.'

The Mahons refused to share information about where members of their family lived in England and claimed to have been told that Melissa had been sighted after 14 September, though they refused to disclose their sources. Their behaviour was simply not helpful.

A number of sightings of Melissa were reported by people who knew her after 14 September 2006, including one on 21 September, four in October and one on 9 March 2007. On 10 October 2006, Yvonne Mahon, Melissa's older sister, told gardaí that she had seen Melissa with Dunbar in his car on the Bundoran Road. Gardaí continued to make surprise visits to Dunbars' house during this time, but found nothing. None of the reported sightings led to Melissa or to any information about where she might be or what may have happened to her.

On 21 September 2006, Maria Lloyd, a part-time member of the social care team in Lis na nÓg, was on a bus on her way into work. She was aware that Melissa had been reported missing a week earlier. She knew Melissa as a resident of the home and she had been asked to keep an eye out for her, even before 14 September, as the girl was often missing and refused to obey the rules. From the window of the bus, Maria noticed a figure running very fast in the direction of the Rathbraughan Estate. It was a girl with a dark hair in a ponytail. She was wearing a pink hooded top and dark tracksuit bottoms. As the bus caught up with the girl, Maria realised that it might be Melissa. There were black stains on the back of the hooded top and Maria recalled similar stains from black hair dye on a top she had previously washed for Melissa.

The girl had her back to Maria the entire time but as she turned down an alleyway, Maria caught a brief glimpse of the side of her face. Maria got off the bus but there were a number of older people getting off in front of her and they held her up. By the time she got to the alleyway, there was no sign of the girl. Maria reported the possible sighting to Judith McLoughlin in Lis na nÓg. She later told the Central Criminal Court that she was 80 per cent certain that the girl she had seen was Melissa Mahon. She could not be sure of the date but her report was noted by Judith in the Lis na nÓg logbook as 21 September.

After Melissa's disappearance, Dunbar told anyone who would listen that he felt that the authorities had failed the girl and were trying to turn him into the scapegoat. He told gardaí that they should be looking to the Mahon family for answers rather than to him. He felt that rumours about his relationship with Melissa were being spread by the Mahons. He would ring Garda Conway to complain and would record their conversations. When cross-examined by Dunbar's barrister in court, Garda Conway said that after Melissa's disappearance, he had spoken to Dunbar on a number of occasions but had often found it difficult to get a word in edgeways. Garda Conway said that, at the time, he had not heard any rumour from any source that Dunbar was having an inappropriate relationship with Melissa.

During the time that Melissa was missing, her sister Leeanna looked through her belongings and found a photograph of Ronnie Dunbar hidden in a red box. Leeanna was so angry she ripped the picture into four pieces and put it in a cupboard in her own room. She later gave it an older sister who handed it over to gardaí on 14 February 2008 after remains, which were strongly suspected to be Melissa's, had been discovered at Lough Gill.

05 | THE TRUTH COMES OUT

Shirley Dunbar was born on 29 June 1990 and was 18 years old when she gave evidence against her father at the Central Criminal Court in April 2009. She had not been present when Melissa Mahon had died, nor was she there when the girl's body had been disposed of.

Her evidence to the court would be about how she came to find out what had happened to Melissa Mahon and how gardaí became involved. Her sister Samantha had broken down in spectacular fashion on 31 January 2008 and had finally told Shirley her awful secret.

Shirley told the court that she had lived with both of her parents in Essex until she had been five years old. Around this time, her mother had left the family home and Shirley and her two younger sisters had remained with their father. When she was 12 years old, he had moved them to Scotland for three years before bringing them to live in his home town of Sligo.

In 2008, Shirley was living with her boyfriend, Danny Lynnott, and their child at 69 Rathbraughan Park, only doors away from the Dunbar family home. When Melissa went missing in September 2006, Shirley was seven months pregnant and living with Danny's mother. She had moved out of her father's house in

January 2006 and had begun a relationship with Danny. She remembered Melissa Mahon from school, but didn't know her as well as her sisters and father did.

She told the court how Samantha and Jill had started hanging around with Melissa and Leeanna Mahon and that they had all been getting into trouble. They regularly skipped school and were eventually suspended. Shirley heard from her father that Melissa was spending all of her time in their house because she was being abused by her parents. Shirley remembered that her sisters and Melissa had played with an Ouija board. Jill had told Shirley that their father had said that they had brought demons and spirits into the house and that the demons were there for Melissa.

One evening in the summer of 2006, another 14-year-old girl who lived in the Rathbraughan Estate went to the Dunbar house to get a cigarette from Ronnie. Samantha and Melissa were in the house when the girl arrived at around 8.30 p.m. She heard them screaming and shouting that there was a ghost in the house. Samantha asked her to call Ronnie and ask him to come home. Later that night, Samantha arrived, barefoot and in tears, at the girl's house. Dunbar's then girlfriend would later tell the court that she had been with Dunbar when he had received that call and that he had run out of her house to perform an 'exorcism' on Melissa.

Shirley also heard a rumour that Melissa was having a relationship with Shirley's boyfriend Danny but told the court, 'It was brought to my attention by my father. I dismissed it. I was pregnant.'

Shirley knew that Melissa had run away from home in August 2006 and she knew that the girl had been hiding in her father's house for the entire three weeks that she was missing. Shirley was a daily visitor at 64 Rathbraughan Park and saw Melissa there during August 2006. Shirley thought the situation was inappropriate and wanted Melissa to leave.

While she was not familiar with the 'ins and outs' of the contact between her father, Melissa and the social workers, she knew that Melissa had been taken into care but still persisted in running away to spend time with her father. When gardaí called to the house looking for Melissa on occasions when Shirley was present, she would hear him blatantly lie that Melissa wasn't there and then say that he would do his best to find her and would keep an ear to the ground.

'I would make it clear that I thought she shouldn't be there. Lis na nÓg would ring him looking for her and he would say she wasn't there and that he would find her and bring her back,' said Shirley.

On the day after Melissa had been placed with a foster family in Kinlough, Shirley heard that the teenager had escaped from the care of her social worker and had, again, gone to the Dunbar house. They had by then moved to 63 Rathbraughan Park but Dunbar still had the key to number 64 and he used it to let Melissa into the empty house. She would climb over the garden wall and use the backdoor key to get into their former home.

By January 2008, Samantha had moved in with Shirley and Danny. On the last day of that month, the two girls were on the phone to their mother in England. They were having a heated conversation with Lisa Conroy during which Samantha became very upset. Shirley was arguing with her mother when Samantha shouted, 'I'll tell you why I'm like this.' Shirley hung up on her mother and sat on the sofa; Samantha was on a chair opposite. Samantha then told her sister that their father had killed Melissa Mahon.

In Shirley's statement to gardaí, she said that when Samantha had offered to explain why she behaved the way she did, she had asked Shirley to swear that she would not tell anyone, because that would get Samantha into big trouble with the gardaí. Shirley also told gardaí that Melissa immediately came into her head when Samantha said she had something to tell her. Shirley said to Samantha, 'She's dead, isn't she?'

Shirley's statement read: 'I said to Sam, "Did Dad kill her?", and she said, "Yeah." I asked her to tell me it was a lie but she said no and became hysterical.' In court, Shirley told her father's barrister that she could not remember the exact words that she had used in her statement but she accepted what it contained.

She also accepted that Samantha shouted, 'I'm going to jail', and was convinced that she and Jill were going to be in a lot of trouble with the gardaí. Shirley said she did not speak to her father after Samantha's revelation but she was told by Kirsty, her half-sister in England, that Jill had given a different version of events to gardaí. Jill claimed that Samantha had attacked Melissa during a camping trip.

During Shirley's time in the witness box, the exhibits officer showed her the nightdress that had been found at the shore of Lough Gill. Shirley confirmed that it was one of two identical nightdresses that had been bought for Samantha and Jill in England when they were younger. The girls had since grown out of them and Shirley had last seen that particular garment in their house in the Rathbraughan Estate. She was then shown the neck tie that gardaí had also found at the lake. She said that it belonged to her father and went on to explain that she had been with him when he had bought it in Scotland and she had last seen it when he had worn it in Sligo the previous Christmas. She remembered it because her father was not a shirt-and-tie man, so it had been unusual to see him wearing one.

Danny Lynnott was with Shirley on the night that gardaí were finally made aware of what had happened to Melissa. He was 21 years old by the time he gave evidence at the Central Criminal Court. He and Shirley had had a son in November 2006 but, by the time of the trial, the couple were no longer together. On 31 January 2008, Danny was in 69 Rathbraughan Park with Shirley, their son and Samantha. At around 6.30 p.m., Danny left to visit his mother who lived nearby. While at his mother's house, he received a voice message from Lisa Conroy. He returned to his own home and played the message on loudspeaker for Shirley and Samantha. It was not a happy message. Lisa was complaining about Samantha, who had spent the previous Christmas with her in England. Lisa wanted Shirley and Danny to know what Samantha had been saying about them.

Lisa had opened a can of worms and the girls rang their mother back. As Danny dressed his son and got ready to go out, the girls fought with Lisa on loudspeaker. Danny and the child escaped the shouting and went to his mother's house. There, he watched the nine o' clock news before heading back to Rathbraughan Park.

When Danny got home, he found chaos. As he approached his front door, he could hear Samantha shouting, 'I'm going to go to jail.' He had forgotten his key so had to knock and wait for Samantha let him in. He was shocked when she appeared. She was absolutely terrified, her hair was all over the place and her eyes were 'burned out from crying'. Shirley had also been in tears and had make-up smeared down her face. Both girls were in an awful state. Danny had never before seen anybody so upset and wanted to know what was wrong. Samantha turned to her sister and asked her if she should tell him. After a few minutes, she managed to blurt out that their father had killed Melissa Mahon. Danny listened as the sisters told him that Ronnie Dunbar had strangled Melissa and put her into a sleeping bag. He had then driven to the River Bonet and dumped her body.

Samantha told Danny that she had come home from Youth Reach at 5 p.m. on a September evening a year and a half earlier. Jill had opened the door that night and had tried to stop Samantha from going upstairs but Samantha had pushed her way past, climbed the stairs and gone into her father's bedroom. There, she had seen her father on the bed with Melissa. His hands had been over Melissa's neck and she had been gasping for air. When her father had seen Samantha, he had jumped up and left the room. Samantha had then unsuccessfully tried to revive her friend. Ronnie had returned with a sleeping bag and had put Melissa into it. He had tied it tightly with a purple neck tie and made the girls help him put the body in the boot of his car. He had then driven all of them to Lough Gill and put Melissa into the water telling his daughters, 'That's Daddy's little secret.' He had told the girls that if they told anyone what had happened, he would go to jail and so would they. They had then gone home and he had burned Melissa's belongings in the fire.

Danny told the court that Dunbar and Samantha would go back out to Lough Gill with binoculars to check if the body had risen and he believed that Dunbar had continued to go out to check until the time of his arrest.

On hearing Samantha's story, Danny wanted to ring the police immediately but Samantha was hysterical and the sisters did not know what to do for the best. Samantha said, 'They'll send me away', and Shirley asked Danny to wait before he did anything. Samantha needed a chance to calm down.

After a few minutes, Danny rang Sligo Garda Station and asked for detectives to come to the house in an unmarked car. He asked for Pauline McDonagh or Con Lee to come and he said that it was in relation to Melissa Mahon, a missing person. Gardaí arrived at the house at 10 p.m.

That night, Danny also learned that Melissa had been pregnant when she disappeared. Shirley told him that she had been with Melissa when she took a pregnancy test, which had been positive. Danny was aware that accusations had been made that he had been seeing Melissa but could not recall whether or not Shirley had confronted him about it. He thought the accusations were circulating long before Melissa had been taken into care or had gone missing. He did not know who was spreading the rumour, though he did not think it was Jill. In any event, he 'passed no heed' to it because there was 'no truth to it'.

At around 10 p.m., Garda Charles Jordan arrived at 69 Rathbraughan Park with Detective Garda Pauline McDonagh. They met Danny at the door and were taken into the front room where they saw Shirley sitting on the sofa and Samantha on an armchair beside the fire. Garda Jordan thought that Samantha looked very frightened. She was staring into space and appeared to be in a trance. Shirley was visibly upset and had obviously been crying.

Detective Garda McDonagh had been on duty in the detective branch since 9.30 p.m. An emergency call had come through for her and, as a result, she had gone to Shirley's house. When she saw Samantha in the armchair, she also thought the girl looked like she was in a trance. She was holding on to the arms of the chair so Detective McDonagh kneeled down beside her to speak quietly to her. She had no idea what was wrong with the girl. Shirley sat opposite them silently holding a string of rosary beads. Danny had to ask Samantha a number of times to tell the detective what was wrong. Eventually, she was able to speak. Samantha told Detective McDonagh that her father had killed Melissa Mahon. She said Ronnie Dunbar had strangled the girl and put her body in a river and that she could bring gardaí to the spot where the body had been dumped. The only other person who knew what had happened was her younger sister, Jill, who had also been present when Melissa had died.

Detective McDonagh knew that Melissa was a missing person and realised that she was in receipt of extremely important information, so she called for superior officers to come to the house. The girls and Danny were taken to Sligo Garda Station and, because of their young ages, arrangements were made for a priest and social workers to come to the station and be with the girls during their interview. Samantha was 16 and Shirley was 17. They were interviewed separately. Samantha gave a lengthy statement in which she repeated what she had already told Detective McDonagh, though she went into much greater detail. She admitted that she had assisted in the disposal of Melissa's body. She continued talking until 4 a.m. when she became too tired to go on.

The independent observers who were called in to be with the girls as they made their statements in the absence of parents and guardians, later told the press that they were disturbed and traumatised by what they heard that night.

Detective McDonagh had known Ronnie Dunbar before that night and had spoken to him on occasion in relation to other issues. At the Central Criminal Court, she agreed with the defence that she went on to have numerous dealings with him after Samantha's statement was made. It was put to her in court that during her most recent interaction with Dunbar, at Castlerea Prison a month before the trial, she had told the accused that he should never have been charged and that the case should never have been brought to court.

'Absolutely, categorically, definitely not,' replied Detective McDonagh. 'I absolutely said no such thing. I would have no reason to make a comment like that.'

She agreed that she had gone to the prison to take a cautioned memo of interview from the accused about whether or not he had been made aware that a court order had been in place barring him from contact with Melissa from 7 September 2006. She was asked by defence counsel if it had been a friendly meeting and she replied, 'I treat everyone with respect, so, yes.'

It was also put to Danny Lynnott during cross-examination that on 6 February 2008, he had rung Sligo Garda Station and spoken to Detective McDonagh. He accepted that he had told the detective that he had information about the case. He had been told by Shirley's older half-sister, Kirsty, that Jill had been saying that Samantha had killed Melissa during a camping trip. According to Jill, she and her father had been present and had assisted Samantha in disposing of the body.

06 | MEDIA FRENZY

S hirley Dunbar went straight to the press with her story. It would turn out that she was not alone in her willingness to talk to the media about what had happened to Melissa Mahon. Many of the people touched by Melissa's death, as well as the chief suspect and those connected to him, would prove themselves far from shy about talking to reporters. The discovery of human remains at a lake coupled with the suspicion that they belonged to a missing teenage girl was obviously going to attract national media attention. Until someone was charged with an offence, the press was at large to print whatever it decided was newsworthy.

Dunbar was not named in early reports but he was described as a sex offender, although he had no previous convictions for sex crimes. Gardaí said at the time that they were 'concerned' about what was being printed. Superintendent Michael Barrett told the press in early February 2008 that the search of Lough Gill was ongoing and he refused to be drawn on any of the claims that had been published. He declined to comment on 'what people put in the newspapers' but renewed the garda appeal for information in relation to Melissa.

The *Sunday World* ran an interview which Shirley gave to Paul Williams in the days following Samantha's revelations. The two-page spread included a family photograph of Dunbar and his three daughters with their faces blurred to hide their identities. The headline ran: 'Smiling Family Photo that Hides a Horrific Tale of Violence, Sick Sex Abuse and Murder'.

In the interview, Shirley told Paul Williams what her sister had told her—that their father had strangled Melissa Mahon, wrapped her body in a sleeping bag and dumped her in a river. It was also claimed that he had been having a sexual relationship with Melissa and that she had become pregnant by him. Other allegations were also published in the newspaper that painted the unnamed suspect in a very poor light. The article would come to play a role in the trial when Dunbar's defence barrister put it to Jill that her version of events was gathered from what she had read in the *Sunday World* rather than from what she had witnessed with her own eyes.

Dunbar, ever the control freak, could not remain silent and approached the *Sligo Weekender* to tell his side of the story. On 12 February 2008, the paper published an interview with the self-proclaimed chief suspect—though he was not identified by name —in which he professed his innocence. He also took the opportunity to deny the other allegations that had been made against him. He claimed to have been interviewed by gardaí for nine hours in October 2007 about those allegations but had been released without charge. He was also horrified that it had been incorrectly reported that he was on the Sex Offenders Register in the United Kingdom.

He told reporter Gerry McLaughlin that he had worked closely with social workers and gardaí to convince Melissa to go into care during the summer prior to her disappearance. After she had gone into care, the Health Service Executive had allowed Melissa to stay in his house during the daytime. Now he felt that the authorities were making him a scapegoat for their failings. Dunbar spoke rapidly and convincingly to the reporter. Those who have dealt with Dunbar have all said that they found it extremely difficult to interrupt him—he likes to control the conversation.

Dunbar used the interview to plant the notion that it was

Samantha who had done something to Melissa. He said that Samantha and Melissa had argued before Melissa's disappearance and showed the reporter a text message purportedly from Jill that alleged that Samantha had hit Melissa over the head with a piece of wood during a fight at the end of September 2006.

He said that he had only ever been concerned for Melissa's safety and absolutely had not murdered her or dumped her body in a lake. He had been contacted by social workers and gardaí to help find Melissa when she had run away from her parents. He boasted that, on one occasion, they had come to his house looking for help and, within half a day, he had been able to get in touch with Melissa. But, later, the tables were turned and gardaí had begun to harass him.

He claimed that by the time she went missing, Melissa was 'out of control' and 'keeping bad company'. He said he last heard from her in the early hours of 14 September 2006, when he had received a phone call in which she had begged him to collect her from a house in Leitrim and bring her home. He had told her he couldn't help her because she was in the care of the authorities. He told the newspaper that, later that morning, he had received a text message from her saying that she was with a social worker and would call him the following day. He claimed that that was the last he had heard from her and it was the gardaí who had informed him the following day that she had run away. He had heard that she was spotted by Health Service Executive Staff on the Old Bundoran Road and he simply could not understand why they hadn't gone after her.

He said that he had been harassed by gardaí for weeks after Melissa's disappearance, even though he had insisted that she was not with him. He had promised the police that he would contact them if she did make an appearance, as he had done many times before. He had been devastated by the accusations that he had harmed her. Dunbar said that he had become very close to Melissa and he had grown genuinely fond of her. She had called him 'Dad'. He believed Samantha had made the accusations against him because she was unwell and had been taking drugs. Why, if he was a murdering paedophile, would he have helped

Melissa in the first place? He continued, 'Why would I have brought her back up the road every time she went missing? Why have I been making enquires ever since then? Surely it would have been in my interests to keep my mouth shut and not be stirring up a hornet's nest. I have a history but I am not a pervert.'

He said that he felt as though he had already been tried and convicted by the media but he still retained a hope that Melissa would show up alive and well. 'It's because I would like to see her again. It's because she did treat me like a dad.'

Niall Delaney, a local journalist working for the Sligo radio station Ocean FM, was as keen as anyone else in the press to get the inside story. He was well aware that Shirley had spoken to the *Sunday World* and that Dunbar had spoken to the local press. Interested in following the story himself, he obtained a phone number for Ronnie Dunbar through his local sources, though he was not able to reveal those sources when questioned in court. When he phoned Dunbar, he asked him if he wanted to respond to the allegations that had been made against him. Dunbar was more than willing, even after giving an interview to the *Sligo Weekender* and they arranged to meet on the afternoon of 19 February 2008.

Dunbar told Niall Delaney that he wanted to 'set the record straight'. They met at 3.30 p.m. at what they decided was a neutral location and sat in Dunbar's car. They spoke for an hour and a half. Dunbar, as usual, had, in advance of the meeting, set out a number of conditions that the reporter had to meet. Their entire conversation had to be recorded. Niall had to speak to Dunbar's youngest daughter, Jill, on the phone and record his conversation with her. Finally, Dunbar's voice had to be disguised in any version of the interview that might be broadcast.

Dunbar told Niall Delaney that he did not kill Melissa Mahon and had had nothing to do with her death. He was very angry and full of complaints about how he was being portrayed in the media. His overriding concern was that his side of the story should be made public. Dunbar talked about his past and how he had been placed in the witness protection programme in England.

His account covered how, when he moved back to Ireland, his daughters had become friendly with Melissa and Leeanna Mahon. He said that the girls, as a group, had begun to get into trouble but that Melissa had started to see Dunbar as a father figure and called him 'Dad' on a regular basis. He was adamant that their relationship was purely that of a father and daughter. He continued that when Melissa had gone into care, she had regularly run away but Dunbar had always contacted the Health Service Executive to tell them where she was. He was looking out for her. The last time he had heard anything from her was on the night that he had received a phone call from a man named Fergus, saying that she was in his house in Leitrim. Melissa had told Mr Fergus that Dunbar was her father. Later, he received a text message from her that had been sent on a social worker's phone, saying that she was safe. That was the end of his contact with Melissa.

Dunbar had watched the reconstruction of Melissa's last known movements on 'CrimeCall'. He could not understand why the two social workers, who had seen her walking along the road after she had left Markievicz House had not gone after her. Niall Delaney asked Dunbar if he had been interviewed by gardaí. He said he had not.

At the beginning of the meeting, Dunbar had handed over his phone to Niall and said that his daughter wanted to speak to him. During that call, the girl gave the journalist a number to call her back on later. Dunbar explained that he wanted his story to get out and she could help with that. Jill and Niall spoke later that day and Niall taped the conversation, but it was never broadcast. He handed over all the recordings to gardaí. Jill had given him an account that involved Samantha and Melissa going on a camping trip during which they had fought. Jill said that Melissa had stolen Samantha's stash of cocaine, so Samantha had hit her across the head with a rock and Melissa had fallen to the ground motionless. Jill said she had witnessed everything and had run away in fright. She said the fight had happened around the time that Melissa went missing and that she hadn't seen Melissa since.

Paul Williams, having spoken to Shirley in early February, was keen to get both sides of the story and arrived at Dunbar's house unannounced later in the month. At the trial, he was listed, alongside Niall Delaney, in the Book of Evidence and both were tendered by the prosecution for cross-examination, but the defence declined to question the *Sunday World*'s crime correspondent.

In what was described in the newspaper as a face-to-face interview with evil, Dunbar had again pleaded his innocence and had made what Paul Williams called 'a series of bizarre allegations'. There had been a brief standoff when the journalist had arrived at the door, but Dunbar had not been able to resist the opportunity to speak to the national press. He invited Paul Williams into his sitting room and started talking.

Dunbar again reiterated his claim that he had been a father figure to Melissa and, once more, pointed the finger of blame at Samantha. He said he was a good parent, even though all of his daughters had by this stage been taken into the care of the Health Service Executive. He said Shirley had made up the story she had earlier given to the paper for two reasons. She was angry because she had seen him with another woman and she wanted revenge because he had thrown her out of his house. The self-proclaimed loving father said Shirley had been taking drugs and having sex with different men.

He argued that if he was a guilty man, then surely he would have already been arrested, but gardaí had not come near him. Samantha had changed her story a number of times and he said that her intimate knowledge of what had happened to Melissa obviously made her a suspect who should be investigated for murder. He said, 'I believe she was there when Melissa was murdered and she knows the full story. I don't know why she is putting it on to me.'

He then claimed that he would be able to point police in the direction of unnamed people who, he said, had murdered Melissa. He said she could have been murdered because she 'knew something' and they wanted to shut her up. Dunbar hypothesised that it suited certain people that he was being blamed. He said, 'All this talk is very dangerous in a town like this. There have been three gangland murders in Sligo in recent years. Someone could come up to my door and put a bullet in my head over this.'

He continued to attack the gardaí because he said they had left him to suffer. He—incorrectly—told Paul Williams that he had never been in trouble with the law in his life, but admitted that he was related to a notorious local family that had been involved in drug offences. Not unlike Mary Mahon, Dunbar blamed Sligo for what had happened to him and his family since his return to his home town.

07 | HE KNEW THIS DAY WOULD COME

Dunbar was eventually arrested on suspicion of Melissa's murder on Thursday, 10 April 2008. Detective Sergeant Padraig Scanlon of the Sligo Detective Branch told the Central Criminal Court that before he arrested Dunbar, he had come into contact with the accused only once—on 25 October 2007 when he had called to Dunbar's home with Garda Pat Conway.

Detective Scanlon said that he had had a conversation with Dunbar on that occasion about where Melissa could possibly be. Dunbar had said that he believed Melissa was in England. He had claimed that he had last heard from her before the date of her disappearance. Dunbar had told the detective, as he had told so many others, that he was angry with the authorities for not dealing with the matter in an appropriate fashion. He had blamed the Health Service Executive and said that the employees who had last spotted Melissa on the street on the day she disappeared had been wrong not to run after her.

Detective Scanlon told the court that warrants to search 63 and 64 Rathbraughan Park were applied for at Sligo District Court on

10 April 2008. As Detective Scanlon was heading out to the estate to arrest Dunbar, he saw a black BMW being driven in the direction of Manorhamilton. He knew this to be Dunbar's vehicle and so activated the siren of his patrol car.

In April 2007, Dunbar had made a deal with an acquaintance, Tom Gettins, to trade his Fiat Cinquecento for an older registration BMW. Mr Gettins told the Central Criminal Court that when he had received the Fiat, it was dirty and badly maintained. The front seats had been broken, the back shelf had been missing and the back seat had been covered in dog hair. Mr Gettins had cleaned the car, changed the hub caps and sold it on.

Dunbar saw the patrol car, pulled over and stepped out of his car, whereupon Detective Scanlon placed a hand on Dunbar's shoulder and informed him that he was under arrest. Dunbar knew that his time was up. This was the moment he had been expecting since Samantha had broken her silence over two months earlier. In court, Detective Scanlon agreed with the defence that the arrest was a carefully planned exercise.

At lunch-time on 10 April 2008, the two houses of interest in Rathbraughan Park were designated crime scenes by Detective Inspector John O'Reilly, the senior investigating officer in the case. Before gardaí could begin the searches, they had to remove Dunbar's six pit bull terriers from the back gardens. Number 63 had a condensation problem. It was poorly ventilated, the heating was on high and it smelled of the dogs. Following the trial, it was reported in the press that the dogs had been put down, something that Dunbar was said to have been furious and deeply upset about.

In number 63, a number of items were found, including a hypodermic syringe and a small bottle marked 'caustic soda', which was on top of a locker in a bedroom. The defence would later apply to the trial judge to prohibit mention of these items to the jury but the prosecution argued that their inclusion would support the credibility of a key witness who had been rigorously cross-examined and attacked for being unreliable. Jill Dunbar told the jury that, in the run-up to his arrest, her father had threatened to commit suicide by injecting himself with caustic soda. The judge decided to allow the jury to hear that the house had contained the equipment Dunbar had told his daughter he would use.

Gardaí also found a deflated inflatable dinghy under a bed. This too would tally with evidence from Jill that months after Melissa's disappearance, her father took her out to the River Bonet on a rubber dinghy in the dead of night to look for Melissa's body.

In number 63, on the windowsills in two bedrooms, gardaí found cardboard boxes with holes cut out and containing miniature binoculars, in the fashion of home-made surveillance units. Material had been cut away from the frame of two divan beds to allow access to the inside of the base. Samantha would tell the court that Dunbar had turned the beds into spaces for Melissa to hide if police arrived at the house looking for her. A search of number 64 revealed nothing of evidential value.

In court, Detective Scanlon was questioned about why Dunbar had not been arrested earlier. Why had he not been questioned on 2 February or shortly after the discovery of human remains at Lough Gill on 11 and 12 February? Detective Scanlon said that they had needed to carry out further investigations and searches and that gardaí had decided to wait until DNA results confirmed that they had found the remains of Melissa Mahon before they arrested anyone.

Gardaí did have Dunbar under surveillance long before his arrest and he was certainly nominated as a suspect after Samantha came forward. Detective Scanlon had called to Dunbar's house on 23 February 2008 after windows had been smashed at the house. Dunbar claimed that he had been threatened but declined to make a complaint.

The defence pointed out that Shirley Dunbar had gone to the *Sunday World* within days of Samantha's story coming to light and accusations about Dunbar had been plastered across two pages of the paper. It was suggested to the detective that gardaí had allowed the investigation to be played out in the national media.

'You were quite happy to simply dangle Ronnie Dunbar out there, let the media get involved and turn this into a circus,' said senior counsel, Brendan Grehan.

Detective Scanlon said he could not accept that. He said the investigation had had to continue, enquiries had to be carried out and the remains had to be identified, all of which took time.

In order to ensure a fair trial after an accused person is charged with an offence, the media is prohibited from commenting on the matter, apart from reporting its progress through the courts. It is an offence, a contempt of court, to publish extraneous material about the accused following a charge and before the matter is finalised. Mr Grehan suggested to Detective Scanlon that the gardaí were happy for this case to unfold in the media before the press was constrained by the arrest and charge of the chief suspect. Mr Grehan alleged that the investigating team knew the media could say what it liked up to the point when Dunbar was charged and gardaí were, therefore, in no hurry to end that situation by arresting him.

Mr Grehan put it to Detective Garda Paul Casey, who was involved in interviewing Dunbar during his detention at Sligo Garda Station, that the investigating team had allowed his client to be pilloried in the newspapers. Dunbar's attitude towards gardaí was, naturally enough, coloured by what he perceived had happened to him in the eight to ten weeks leading up to his arrest. Detective Casey responded that the gardaí had had no control over what the newspapers had printed.

Mr Grehan said of the period between the search of Lough Gill and his client's arrest, 'Perhaps gardaí hoped that my client would top himself or someone else would top him or he would simply come in and put his hands up.'

The defence argued that this was a method employed against Dunbar to 'soften him up'. Detective Casey replied that gardaí were simply conducting a 'methodical investigation'.

On 10 April, Dunbar was cautioned and taken to Sligo Garda Station at around 11 a.m. He consented to gardaí taking his fingerprints, palm prints and photographs. A mobile phone and a Dictaphone were found in his possession. Garda Colin Duffy, the member in charge—the garda responsible that day for ensuring that the detention of an arrested person was conducted in a legal and fair manner—made Dunbar aware of his rights and contacted the solicitor that Dunbar requested. Just after midday, a text came through to Dunbar's phone from Jill which read: 'I don't f***ing care, I f***ing love you and care for you and I hope you are ok.'

Dunbar met with his solicitor before he was brought to an interview room by Detective Sergeant Dermot Flannery and Detective Garda Casey. Dunbar refused to select the video which would be used to record the interview, leaving the member in charge to do so. He would later refuse to sign any of the four written memos of interview. Jill was informed that her father had been detained and she rang the station the following day to find out how he was. During the afternoon of his first day of detention, Dunbar's only concern was for the welfare of his dogs.

At the outset of the first interview, Dunbar told the detectives, 'I've been waiting some time for this.' He was asked how he had come to know Melissa Mahon and replied, 'Just read the newspapers.' He accused gardaí of allowing the press to abuse and attack him.

During this interview Dunbar denied that Melissa had slept in his home on a regular basis. He said she had not slept in his house during the summer of 2006, in fact, she had never stayed over. 'Just because people say it does not mean that it is true,' he said. 'She never slept in my house. Give me dates.' He was asked if Mary Mahon and her daughter Leeanna had called to his home in August 2006 and he replied, 'You mean the time she beat the shit out of Melissa and gave her a back hander?' He told the detectives to ask Mary about 'the abuse that child suffered'.

He was asked if he remembered being confronted by Mary's sister, Anne, and said, 'She told me to give the Mahons a wide berth. If I was a murderer, I wouldn't be drawing attention to myself. Why would I ring social workers and gardaí every time Melissa went missing?' He then accused Melissa of disappearing with a young man named Danny Mills. He said that the two had been drinking and taking drugs. 'I was trying to get her out of harm's way. I got her to go into care. She didn't trust the social workers and she was right.'

During the trial, Danny Mills was called by the prosecution to give evidence about his alleged relationship with Melissa. A witness summons was issued for him but he refused point blank to come to court. The prosecution successfully applied for a bench warrant that allowed gardaí to bring him to the hearing. He then told the jury that he had known Melissa for three days in 2006. He thought her mother lived on a street where he and a friend had been hanging around. He denied that he ever had a relationship with her.

Sarah (not her real name) was another teenage girl who gave evidence at the trial. She said that she had been friends with Melissa and had believed that Melissa had been seeing Danny before her disappearance.

Danny lived in the Caltragh Estate and he knew Sarah as she had hung around the estate once or twice. However, he said that he had no idea how Sarah could have thought that he was seeing Melissa. On the third and final time that Danny had seen Melissa, he saw gardaí putting her into a squad car on the Caltragh Estate. Danny said that he knew nothing about Melissa being taken out of a house where she had been found with a number of young men. Following her disappearance, Danny had been interviewed by gardaí about whether or not he had had a relationship with Melissa. He had told the gardaí the same thing that he later told the court. It simply had not happened.

During his interview, gardaí questioned Dunbar about the meeting with Melissa in Slish Wood to which he had taken Catherine Farrelly. He said he had no idea how Melissa had managed to get to the woods on that day. Dunbar's then girlfriend, Angelique Sheridan, had told garda that he had orchestrated the whole thing and that she had taken Melissa to the woods as directed by him. Dunbar denied this. 'I was trying to get her off the streets. If the social workers had done their job right I wouldn't be here now.'

When he was accused of manipulating Melissa's vulnerability, Dunbar said that he could not see how that was the case. 'I was helping her. I am not going to be made a scapegoat.' He agreed that she was often in his car but said that was because he took her 'out and about' to get her away from trouble in the town. Asked how he would locate her when she went missing, he replied sarcastically, 'It's called making phone calls.' He claimed that when Melissa could not be found, you could be sure that she would be with Danny Mills or another young man.

'We had a father–daughter relationship. It was platonic. I barred her from my house when I found out she had been robbing.' When accused of having a sexual relationship with Melissa, his response was, 'You're reading too many papers.'

Questioned about why he had not just left the social workers to care for Melissa, Dunbar said that it was the social workers who had involved him in her life further by ringing him to collect her.

He said that when social workers wanted to talk to him about Melissa he had gone to Lis na nÓg where he had seen a teenage boy who was also resident at the home. Dunbar said he had words with the boy, whom, he claimed, had kicked his dog and had been smoking marijuana with Samantha and Melissa. Dunbar said he told the social workers that the boy had been trying to have sex with Melissa and had been slipping in and out of her bedroom in Lis na nÓg. He claimed that Melissa had told his daughters that she had had sex with the boy. But he told gardaí that when he reported that information to the social workers, they had done nothing about his complaints.

During questioning, Dunbar said that Melissa was a rebel, 'She was clever and articulate. She knew how to play people.' He said she was openly affectionate with him and was looking for a father figure as she had had 'a rough time' at home with her own family. 'They treated her like an animal,' he said. He accused Mary Mahon of beating Melissa so badly the morning Melissa was found hiding with Samantha in his shed that Melissa had urinated before Mary had dragged her out of his house by her hair.

He also told gardaí that when he had been in hospital, Melissa had slept in his bed in his house in Rathbraughan with the teenage boy from Lis na nÓg and another female resident of the home. He said he did not know who had slept in his bed on the nights that he was with Angelique Sheridan.

Dunbar told gardaí that his youngest daughter, Jill, would be able to 'clear up the situation'. He called Samantha's version of events a 'fairy tale' and denied that he had used his daughters to help carry Melissa's body. He denied that he was now hiding behind his girls and attempting to implicate them.

Detectives put it to Dunbar that Jill's statements, which gave various versions of events mostly blaming Samantha for Melissa's death, were a misguided attempt by her to remove him from blame and that she was attempting to protect him because of the level of control and influence he had over her. Dunbar retaliated by asking, 'If she's in care now, how can I have control over her?'

That evening, Detective Sergeant Peter Kenny of the National Bureau of Criminal Investigation took a written note of a further interview with Dunbar, during which he claimed that the last time he had seen Melissa was the weekend before she disappeared, when she had thrown a birthday present for him over the wall of his back garden after he had refused to let her into the house for his party. The last time he had heard from her, by his account, was the late-night phone call he had received from Hugh Fergus and then the text he had received from Melissa from the social worker's phone. It was put to him that records showed that his mobile phone had made seven phone calls and had sent a number of text messages to Melissa's phone between midnight on 13 September 2006 and just before 11 a.m. the following morning. He said he did not make the calls and that Samantha may have had his phone at that time.

He acknowledged that he had read the interview that Shirley had given to the *Sunday World* about what Samantha had said had happened. He again said that Samantha's version of events was a fiction and that he knew for a fact that Samantha was using drugs.

'Do you love your daughter?' he was asked.

'No.'

'Are you a murderer?'

'No.'

'Admit what you did. Be a man.'

'No.'

Gardaí then changed tack somewhat and asked Dunbar about his routine in the gym but he was awkward and uncooperative to the last. He said he did not know what he did when he was at the gym. Asked how much he could bench press, he replied that he did not know what that meant.

All the detectives who were involved in questioning Dunbar during his detention were cross-examined during the trial about the role the press had played in the investigation. They accepted that the press had had a huge interest in the case but that the garda attitude was that they did not and could not police the newspapers and, therefore, could not be in any way responsible for what had been printed.

Detective Sergeant Flannery agreed that, during the first interview, Dunbar was more than keen to talk about his view that he had been hung out to dry by the media and had been denied due process. However, Detective Sergeant Flannery pointed out that many of the interviews that had been given to the press had been at the behest of Dunbar himself.

Mr Justice White rhetorically remarked during the cross-examination of one of the detectives in relation to the press, 'Would you pay any attention to certain tabloid newspapers?'

The day after Dunbar's questioning by Detectives Casey and Flannery saw him providing even less co-operation. His mantra became, 'I've given you a full account and I am an innocent man.' It was what he said when presented with the sleeping bag that had been found on 13 February 2008 along the shoreline of Lough Gill and was his stock response to each of the following questions. 'Did you purchase the sleeping bag?' 'Is this the sleeping bag into which you put Melissa's body?' 'Why did you dispose of two similar sleeping bags?' 'Is this the bag we recovered as a result of information given to us by your daughter?'

He told the detectives to keep the sleeping bag at a distance from him. 'Make sure that is kept well away from me. I don't want my DNA getting on that bag. I don't want you fitting me up for murder.' He was shown the neck tie and nightdress that had also been found at the lake and, again, responded that he had absolutely nothing to say about the items. 'You sit there convinced that you've destroyed all evidence,' remarked Detective Sergeant Flannery.

The detective accused Dunbar of preying on Melissa and feeding her 'rubbish' about the 'new world' and 'demons', while, at the same time, allowing and encouraging her to become infatuated with him. Dunbar remained unmoved and warned his inquisitors, 'I'll sit here and give you the silent treatment.'

He was asked about instructing Niall Delaney from Ocean FM to interview Jill who, at the time, was 15 years old but he would not be drawn on that specific issue and, instead, talked about the different versions of events Jill had given to the police compared with what Samantha had said. He warned the detectives, 'I can see that any solicitor will wipe the floor with those conflicting statements.' He broke away from his parrot-like assertion of innocence to talk, out of nowhere, about the woman he had been seeing before Melissa disappeared. 'I want to say that Angelique Sheridan got engaged after we split up', and then he claimed that any evidence against him was circumstantial.

Angelique Sheridan had told the police that she had heard Dunbar say that he planned to kill Melissa. That accusation was put to him and he replied, 'I certainly did not.'

'You murdered her because she was pregnant with your child. Your interest in her was sexual.'

Dunbar, quite the legal expert, replied, 'That's hearsay. If you have evidence put it to me.'

Gardaí suggested to Dunbar that he was jealous of the teenage boy who was a resident in Lis na nÓg. Again, they accused him of getting Melissa pregnant. He replied, 'Prove that. Don't give me any more hearsay. I didn't kill anyone. I didn't carry anyone in the boot of my car and I didn't strangle anyone.' Asked if Melissa's death had been an accident, he said, 'Please listen to me, I did not have sex with Melissa Mahon.' He said that Angelique Sheridan's account of how Melissa got to Slish Wood was untrue. He was asked a second time if Melissa's death was an accident and said, 'I haven't got a clue. I wasn't there.'

Samantha's statement was read to Dunbar but his attitude remained the same. 'I think I've given you as many answers as I'm going to. Cut to the chase.'

He was then quizzed about the number of calls and texts between his phone and Melissa's mobile in the month leading up to her disappearance. He said that Samantha was always 'robbing' his phone and added, 'You do your investigation and I'll do mine.'

At trial, Detective Sergeant Flannery said under cross-examination that, during the four interviews, Detective Garda Casey had been taking a written note. Mr Grehan suggested that some of his client's denials had been left out of the memos. Detective Sergeant Flannery said that he had not watched the video of interview, so could not comment but it was often difficult to note every single word spoken during an interview. Mr Grehan said that, in the video, the last question his client was asked was 'Did you do it?', to which he replied, 'No, I did nothing', and that that exchange had not been included in the written note.

Mr Grehan asked the detective if it was fair to say that, at all stages, Dunbar had said nothing about his daughters, to which Detective Sergeant Flannery replied, 'It's fair to say he was very clever about how he answered questions.' He agreed that Dunbar had refused to comment on the specifics of his daughters' versions of events and had told gardaí to go back and ask the girls, rather than him, about what they had said.

Garda Duffy, the member in charge, was also cross-examined by Mr Grehan and was asked if Dunbar had complained about being abused off camera at any time during his detention. Garda Duffy said he did not recall anything of that nature but was aware that Dunbar had felt uncomfortable with the manner and line of questioning.

At the conclusion of the second day of interviews, Dunbar was charged with the murder of Melissa Mahon and brought before a special sitting of Sligo District Court. By the time he was taken to the courthouse across the road, a number of people had converged on the garda station.

Detective Inspector John O'Reilly told the court that Gerry McGovern, Dunbar's solicitor, had asked him to walk Dunbar across to the courthouse but he had refused. He instead took Dunbar across the road by car, having decided that, in Dunbar's own interests, it was not appropriate or safe to transport him on foot.

The media had learned from the Garda Press Office that Dunbar had been arrested and detained and journalists would know how long he could be held before he had to be released or charged.

Detective Inspector O'Reilly told Mr Grehan that he believed that there had been a group of perhaps 20 or 30 people outside the garda station. Mr Grehan said that his client instructed him that it was more like an angry mob of around a hundred people.

At the time, the *Sligo Weekender* reported that up to 200 people had attacked the unmarked garda car in which Dunbar was driven to the court just after 8 p.m. on Friday, 11 April. The paper said that the hostile scenes involved a large number of teenagers, friends and neighbours of Melissa, who were throwing abuse and eggs at the vehicle—a garda was reported to have been hit in the face by an egg.

When charged, Dunbar replied, 'Nothing to say.' Judge Oliver McGuinness, who had, in 2006, made an order prohibiting contact between Dunbar and Melissa, remanded him in custody and granted an application for free legal aid. As Dunbar was driven to Castlerea Prison, spectators thumped the car and shouted 'murderer'.

As Dunbar had been charged, the media was now restricted and could only print that which emanated from the court proceedings. On 28 October 2008, the case was listed at the Central Criminal Court in Dublin and Mr Justice Paul Carney set 20 April 2009 as the date for trial.

08 | TRIAL OPENS

On Monday, 20 April 2009, a year and 10 days after Dunbar had been arrested, a jury was sworn in at the Central Criminal Court for his trial.

Each Monday morning of the court term, members of the public who have received jury summonses crowd into the back of courtroom one in the Round Hall of the Four Courts in front of Mr Justice Paul Carney.

Dunbar, dressed in casual sports clothing, was brought in and stood as the charges were read out in the presence of all potential jurors. He was charged on count one that, on a date unknown between 14 and 30 September 2006 within the county of Sligo, he murdered Melissa Mahon. Count two charged him that, during the same period and in the same place, he made a threat to kill or cause serious harm to Samantha Conroy—his daughter had decided to take her mother's name. Dunbar pleaded not guilty to both counts. Six men and six women were selected to try him. They were informed that the trial would begin the following day before Mr Justice Barry White and was estimated to last five weeks. The prosecution barristers would be Isobel Kennedy sc and Sean Gillane bl and Dunbar would be defended by Brendan Grehan sc and Joseph Barnes bl.

At any trial, the members of the jury are first instructed to elect a foreman from among their number by whatever means they might choose. There is no formula laid down for how a jury should reach any decision it is asked to make and the members are at large to determine how they will operate in all matters. What goes on between the members of the jury within the jury room is entirely private.

The foreman has the role of speaking for the jury as a whole and of communicating to the court any questions or difficulties that might arise during their deliberations.

On Tuesday morning, the long-awaited trial began with the prosecution's opening statement.

Mary and Frederick Mahon were there along with their daughter, Leeanna, and several other family members. Dunbar took up his position on the bench opposite the jury which he shared with prison officers and members of the press.

At no time during a trial should the jury see the accused being led into or out of the courtroom by prison officers. Neither should the accused be seen in handcuffs by the jury. That rule also prohibits the media from publishing photographs of the accused in chains being led to or from a prison van. The fact of an accused person's imprisonment is withheld from the jury in order to preserve the presumption of innocence. Nothing that could prejudice the jury's opinion of the accused, other than the evidence properly given in court, should be available to its members. Previous convictions, should they exist, are not disclosed to the jury during the trial unless exceptional circumstances arise.

The prosecution is prohibited from presenting evidence of an accused person's bad character or criminal record. Such evidence is considered to be extremely prejudicial. It is believed that if an accused person has been found guilty of crimes previously, a jury may be more willing to accept that he or she is guilty of the current alleged offence, even if it is not convinced of it beyond a reasonable doubt. However, there are exceptions to this rule. Previous bad character may be revealed if its probative value outweighs its prejudicial effect—for example, a jury may be allowed to hear about previous convictions that are so similar in character that they show the accused to have a particular modus operandi, though there must be striking similarities between the previous offence and the current allegation before the trial judge would deem the evidence to be admissible. Dunbar did have a slew of previous convictions but they were largely for theft-type offences and were inadmissible. The details would only be heard by the trial judge at sentencing in the event of a conviction.

The opening speech by the prosecution fulfils a number of functions. It sets out the differing roles of the participants in the trial, explains the fundamental principles of law, which should be at the forefront of the jury's mind, and provides a synopsis or overview of the evidence that the prosecution will present. The jury is told that prosecution barristers appear on behalf of the Director of Public Prosecutions, who has charged the accused with the offences on behalf of the State and the people of Ireland. The prosecution's role is not to secure a conviction at all costs but, rather, to lay the evidence fairly before the jury.

Barristers for the defence then test that evidence through cross-examination. The jury must be satisfied beyond a reasonable doubt by the prosecution's case before it may convict the accused. The jury has sole responsibility for deciding what the facts in the case are and no one may trespass on that function. The trial judge's role is to play referee in arguments between the prosecution and defence and have the final word in determining what the law is. The jury has dominion over the facts but it must take directions in relation to the law from the judge.

The concept of the presumption of innocence is also explained to the jury at this stage of the trial. The burden of proving the case against the accused lies, at all times, with the prosecution. The defence need prove nothing. It is for the State to satisfy the jury of guilt and the accused is presumed to be innocent up and until a jury decides otherwise.

Ms Kennedy, having explained the usual matters, told the members of the jury in brief what they would hear during the course of the trial. She told them to be careful not to take what she said during her opening speech as evidence. Only what the jury hears from witnesses in the witness box can amount to evidence.

The jury was told that Melissa Mahon had moved to Sligo with her family in the summer of 2005 and had become friendly with the accused man's daughters. She had spent a great deal of time in the Dunbar house and had run away from her own home the following summer. Social workers and gardaí had become involved in looking for her and she had, eventually, been taken into the care of the Health Service Executive. She went missing again in September 2006. Despite some reported sightings that came to nothing, Melissa's fate was not known until February 2008 when the partner of one of the accused man's daughters contacted gardaí with information.

In this opening speech, the jury heard that the accused man's daughters would testify for the prosecution that they had seen him kill Melissa Mahon and dump her body in a river. Samantha Dunbar, the daughter he had allegedly threatened to kill, would tell the jury how she had seen her father on a bed with Melissa with his arm around her neck before he tied her into a sleeping bag, drove to a secluded area and threw her into a river.

The first witnesses to be called in a trial are usually the gardaí who photographed the crime scenes and created maps of the relevant areas. They set the scene for the jury. Detective Garda Mairead Crowley had photographed the inside of 63 Rathbraughan Park on 10 and 11 April 2008 following Dunbar's arrest. The jury was shown photographs taken of newspaper clippings from the *Sligo Champion* and the *Sligo Weekender*. They were articles about Melissa's disappearance and bore the headlines: 'Garda Appeal Re Missing Girl' and 'Come Home Darling Says Tearful Mum'. They had been found in a plastic shopping bag in the living room of the house. Photographs were also shown of the binoculars hidden in cut-out cereal boxes that had been found on the windowsills of two upstairs bedrooms and of the inflatable dinghy under the bed in the box room.

Detective Garda Laura Bolger had produced maps for the jury of the area around the River Bonet and Lough Gill that the prosecution said were the locations where Melissa's body had been disposed of and later found. The 17.5-kilometre route between Rathbraughan Park and the point of entry at the riverbank was displayed on the maps given to the jury. The maps indicated that the area at the edge of the lake over which items relevant to the case had been found stretched 25 metres along the shoreline and two to three metres inland from the water's edge. The jury was also given plans of both the houses in Rathbraughan Park in which the accused had lived.

As witnesses were called, a picture of Melissa's last weeks began to emerge. Mary, Frederick and Leeanna Mahon gave their evidence followed by Catherine Farrelly. Mr Grehan cross-examined each witness thoroughly, trying to pick holes in what they had said, find inconsistencies or elucidate more information about the background to the case than they had given in their direct evidence. During the trial, Mr Grehan remarked to Mr Justice White, in the absence of the jury, that his client had taken the position that he was not going to read any documents relating to the case in advance of the evidence being given in court.

This led to a rather strange situation where Dunbar—dressed always in a tight, short-sleeved T-shirt, that drew attention to the many tattoos on his arms, and tracksuit bottoms—would sit with paper and pen furiously scribbling reams of notes as witnesses spoke. A constant flow of hand-written missives flew from his hand to his solicitor, who then brought them to Mr Grehan's attention, often while he was on his feet in the middle of a cross-examination. Dunbar carried his pages of notes to and from the courtroom in a plastic shopping bag. His attitude clearly seemed to be that rather than give an explanation about what might have happened between him and Melissa, the best defence would be to poke holes in what other people had to say. He appeared to think that clever barristers would be able to show up witnesses as liars and, thereby, make it impossible for a jury to convict him.

The defendant is in no way obliged to raise a positive defence, give their side of any story or prove any point. They can sit back and insist that the prosecution proves its case beyond a reasonable doubt. Dunbar's strategy was to put the prosecution 'on proof', which even required that the State carefully prove the process by which Melissa's remains had been identified. Often, the prosecution and defence will agree certain matters in advance of the trial, or during it, to narrow the issues and save time and expense. Agreements are often reached on matters that are not in contention and that provide no benefit for the defence to test. The only aspect of the State's case that it was not required to prove, because the defence accepted that there was no issue in relation to it, was the garda preservation of the scene at Lough Gill.

As well as passing innumerable notes to his legal team during the hearing, Dunbar often wanted to instruct them verbally about how he wanted the questioning to proceed. Mr Justice White later remarked that he had given the defence wide latitude in both the actual manner and scope of the cross-examinations and in the number of times he had allowed the hearing to be interrupted to enable Dunbar to instruct his team further.

An example of how bizarre some of Dunbar's instructions were came on a day when what appeared to be an entire football team from Sligo descended on the Four Courts. It was the 17th day of the trial, and Jill and Samantha had already told the court that after their father had killed Melissa and thrown away her body, he had attended his regular football practice and had brought them along with him as though nothing unusual or untoward had happened. Francis Lyons was a member of the group of men who practised together every Thursday at the Teeling Sports Centre in Collooney. He told the court that Dunbar always brought his daughters to the training sessions and that the group always played on a Thursday night between 7 p.m. and 8 p.m. He said that Dunbar's daughters were noisy. They wore heavy eye make-up and would often squabble. They stood out because it was unusual that teenage girls would be brought along to a men's football practice, but the Dunbar girls were always there as though they were attached to their father's hip. Several other men gave very similar evidence and their point seemed very well made. Dunbar played football on a Thursday night.

More unusual than the sheer volume of this evidence was a line of questioning adopted by Mr Grehan about a friend of Dunbar's called Big Mick.

Mr Grehan, having been instructed to do so, asked the footballers if they remembered a party that had been held in a Sligo pub for Big Mick's birthday two years earlier. Had they attended? Was Ronnie Dunbar there? Had they spent time with Dunbar at that gathering? Witnesses and observers seemed bemused by the questions. What did this have to do with Melissa Mahon? None of the men seemed to remember spending much time with Dunbar at the party. Mr Grehan accused Jonathan Sweeney of trying to distance himself from Dunbar by refusing to admit that he had ever socialised with his client. Mr Sweeney denied that this was the case and said that he had only stayed in the pub for a short time.

Eventually, Mr Justice White, in the absence of the jury, remarked to Mr Grehan that his cross-examination was heading down an entirely irrelevant avenue and should be curbed. He wanted to know if Mr Grehan was trying to make it appear to the jury that Dunbar was like any other ordinary man who went to the pub and socialised with other people and therefore not a murderer? The judge saw it as a fruitless exercise.

After the lunch break, the mood had darkened between Mr Grehan and his client. Before the jury was brought out, and just as everyone else settled in for another afternoon of evidence, Mr Grehan informed Mr Justice White that he had a professional difficulty and would not be able to continue unless and until the matter was resolved. The jury members were told that a matter had arisen that had to be dealt with in their absence and they were sent home for the remainder of the day.

Communications between a lawyer and his or her client are privileged and it is not known exactly what went on between Dunbar and Mr Grehan that afternoon, but it certainly appeared that tension had arisen between them.

As though his physical appearance was not enough of a hindrance, Dunbar's behaviour and demeanour throughout the trial also gained him no sympathy. Mr Justice White would later remark at the sentence hearing that he had little doubt that Dunbar had proved to be one of Mr Grehan's most difficult clients.

Observers waited anxiously to hear what would happen next. If Mr Grehan withdrew as defence counsel, some doubted that Mr Justice White would be willing to abandon the trial at this advanced stage; especially not in circumstances where the difficulty had perhaps arisen because of the attitude of the defendant. There was speculation that maybe time would be given to enable Dunbar to instruct new counsel so that the trial could continue after a hiatus of a few days or a week. The trial was already taking up the entire court term and there had, from the outset, been a danger that it could spill over into the court holidays. Mr Justice White had warned participants from the start that if the trial was not completed within the court term, it would sit through the break. Sitting through the holiday may have become inevitable had Mr Grehan's professional difficulty not been resolved. Whatever happened overnight, Mr Grehan told the court the following morning that he was in a position to continue. The crisis had been averted.

During the lengthy trial, the jury heard from many witnesses who provided background information or confirmed details such as how Melissa's remains had been gathered and examined, and when and where Dunbar had played football. The meat of the evidence—and what would ultimately scupper Dunbar's hopes of walking free—was the testimony of the women in his life.

He had made a lifetime habit of controlling and manipulating women who were too young or too vulnerable to defeat his will. Those women chose the Central Criminal Court to be the forum where they finally stood up to him.

09 | ANGELIQUE SHERIDAN

Angelique Sheridan, née Dubois, was Dunbar's girlfriend during the period leading up to Melissa's disappearance. She gave evidence for the prosecution on the third day of his trial and was examined by Mr Gillane. She had been born in London and had moved to Ireland when she was 21 years old and lived in Sligo. She had two children, a boy and a girl.

She first met Dunbar in Sligo General Post Office in the early days of August 2006. She was in the company of her young daughter and Ronnie was, as always, with his two youngest girls. The adults fell into conversation in the queue and then Angelique left the post office and went about her business. She went into a chemist and was followed by Samantha and Jill. In an unorthodox pick up, the sisters approached Angelique and handed over their father's phone number which he had scribbled on a piece of paper. Angelique was surprised but took the number and then took her daughter to McDonald's. As the pair were sitting by the window eating their food, Angelique spotted Dunbar walking past. He waved to her from the street.

Dunbar had made an impression and, that evening, Angelique took a chance and decided to contact him. She sent a text message saying that she would be happy to go out on a date. He rang her back immediately and they made arrangements for Dunbar to pick her up at her flat on Wolfe Tone Street.

A day or two later, Angelique was preparing for her date and was dressed up ready to go out, however, when Dunbar arrived in his little blue car, Samantha and Jill were also with him. Alarm bells should have started to ring for Angelique, but they didn't and she welcomed Dunbar and his daughters into her home before making tea for everyone. Then, Dunbar formally introduced his girls to the confused single mother.

It was a lovely summer's evening and he suggested a spin in his car out to Slish Wood, so Angelique, her daughter, Dunbar, Samantha and Jill all went for a drive. They took her car—his was too small to fit everyone comfortably. After the drive, they stopped at Lidl to buy wine and pizzas and Dunbar and his daughters stayed at Angelique's flat until 11 p.m. or midnight. At the end of their first 'date', Dunbar and Angelique agreed to meet again and he texted her the following day. Angelique told the court that a relationship developed quickly and they began to meet on a daily basis. She said that his youngest daughter, Jill, had taken a particular shine to her and had clung to her from the beginning. Angelique was later introduced to Dunbar's elder daughter, Shirley, who was pregnant at the time.

Two weeks into the budding romance, Dunbar first mentioned to Angelique a young girl whom, he said, was being abused by her father and beaten by her mother. He said the teenager was looking to him for protection. He told his new girlfriend that he had seen the girl's mother punching her daughter in the face when she had been found hiding in his garden shed with Samantha. Angelique told Dunbar that she thought the appropriate course of action would be for him to go to the gardaí or speak to a social worker.

Dunbar introduced Angelique to Melissa at a picnic in Slish Wood. Angelique's daughter was there and Dunbar had brought Samantha, Jill and Melissa. Melissa was shy and taciturn and didn't make any conversation with Angelique. She kept very close to Samantha and appeared to get along exceptionally well with Dunbar. Angelique began to sense that something was amiss.

Dunbar had previously been 'a proper gentleman' and had lavished Angelique with attention but, on the day of the picnic, his focus was entirely on the teenage girls. 'He didn't pass much heed to me,' she told the court. The girls were moody and the usually affectionate Dunbar had little or no time for Angelique.

The picnic took place during the time that Melissa was missing from her own family home in August 2006. Angelique was aware that Dunbar was in touch with Garda Pat Conway about Melissa's disappearance and knew that, although Melissa was staying in Dunbar's house, he was telling gardaí that he did not know where she was and that he had only had telephone contact with her.

Dunbar tried to assuage Angelique's concerns about the situation by telling her that Melissa had not made a written statement to gardaí about the abuse she was suffering at home. Dunbar told Angelique that if he betrayed Melissa and revealed her whereabouts to gardaí, she would be taken back to her parents and subjected to further abuse. He was protecting her from harm. Angelique bought his story.

Angelique believed that Melissa didn't like her very much, despite the older woman's best efforts to be friendly and make her feel comfortable. Angelique cooked for Melissa and tried to engage her in conversation but with little success. She had believed Dunbar's story about parental abuse and felt sorry for the teenager. She noticed that Samantha and Melissa were extremely close, to the exclusion of Jill, and often walked with their arms linked. Angelique told the court that Jill had claimed that Melissa and Samantha had sometimes beat her up and that Jill had received a text message saying that Melissa was going to stab her.

Matters took a more sinister turn when Dunbar involved Angelique in his plan to hoodwink social services into meeting with Melissa without revealing that she had been in his house for the entire time that she had been reported missing. Dunbar managed to convince Angelique to surreptitiously bring Melissa to Slish Wood to meet Catherine Farrelly. Angelique had thought that it was a good thing that Dunbar was involving the social services in Melissa's case. She told the court, 'When I agreed to the plan, he brought Melissa to my flat in the boot of his car.' Melissa was hidden under a tartan blanket in the car and when they arrived, she had jumped out of the boot on Wolfe Tone Street and had run into Angelique's home. Dunbar also brought blow-up beds so that he, Melissa, Samantha and Jill could spend that night in Angelique's flat.

The teenagers were to sleep on the sitting-room floor while Dunbar was to stay in Angelique's room. Before everyone went to bed, Angelique waited for Dunbar to leave the room and then took the opportunity to speak to the girls. Melissa told Angelique that she believed she was the reincarnation of Cleopatra and that Ronnie was her reincarnated lord. She believed that they had been in love and had been married in a previous life and would be reunited when the new world order came. When that day arrived, they would move to the highlands to live together as husband and wife. When they died, they would be burned together on boats that would be floated down a river.

Samantha told Angelique that she could see ghosts but that she was protected by her father, whom she believed was a demon fighter who could catch evil spirits in the tattoos on his arms.

Angelique was gobsmacked by the girls' ravings. She confronted Dunbar about what she had learned. Surely these were the notions of disturbed and overly imaginative girls. About Melissa in particular she said to him, 'My God, this little girl needs help.' However, Dunbar's reaction was far from what she had expected. He said that, of course, it was possible that Melissa had been reincarnated. He could not see what was wrong with such a belief and perhaps Samantha could see ghosts. He told Angelique that everyone had, and was entitled to, their beliefs. He was completely calm about what the girls had said. Teenagers believed such things and he could not see the harm in it. Angelique had a different opinion.

At 7 a.m. the next day, everyone was waking up. Angelique was still very confused and disturbed by what she had learned. She had agreed to Dunbar's plan to bring Melissa to a social worker because she had believed that the girl needed help, but the previous night's conversations had worried her deeply and she knew that something was seriously wrong with the situation. She confronted Dunbar again and told him that Melissa would have to make a statement to gardaí about her father. She needed real and professional help and the only way she was going to be able to get it was by going to the authorities.

Angelique did not realise that Melissa was listening in to her conversation with Dunbar. When the teenager flew into a rage and began shouting, Dunbar immediately took her side and said he would not force her to make any statement against her will. Jill then became involved in the row and announced that Melissa was in love with Dunbar.

Gauging Angelique's reaction, Dunbar covered up. He told his girlfriend that Melissa had developed a crush on him—a childish infatuation—but that she was over it. Now, she saw him only as a father figure. He said that Melissa had been barred from his house at an earlier stage because of the notion she had taken for him. At this point, Melissa had heard enough and, unable to take any more, ran out of Angelique's flat. Dunbar raced after her and quickly brought her back inside.

When everyone had calmed down, attention returned to the day's purpose. It was time to carry out the carefully orchestrated plan to facilitate a meeting between Melissa and Catherine Farrelly without revealing Dunbar's true role in the girl's life.

He gave Angelique strict instructions. She was to bring Jill and Melissa in her car to Slish Wood, drop Melissa at a picnic bench in a clearing where she would park and then take Jill and stay out of sight. The girls set off and Angelique did as she was told. She drove to the woods and left Melissa alone at the bench to wait for Dunbar. Angelique took Jill to a hilly area where they would not be spotted, but from where they were able to observe what would happen. Soon, Dunbar arrived in his car with Samantha and the social worker. Angelique was again surprised as she had believed a garda would also be at the meeting. She watched for the next half an hour as the meeting took place. When Dunbar, Samantha and the social worker had driven away and were safely out of the area, Angelique returned to collect Melissa.

She had been instructed to return to her flat, wait outside and text Dunbar to let him know that they had arrived home. Dunbar dropped Catherine back to her office and returned to Angelique's with Samantha. Outside the flat, Melissa jumped into his boot and Dunbar covered her with the blanket again and drove away.

Two days later, Dunbar phoned Angelique and told her that he was sick and needed to go into hospital for an operation. He told her he had got blood poisoning from a bite. When she visited him in hospital, he told her that the demons had to get out somehow. She had hoped that such talk was because of the effects of the anaesthetic. At the hospital, she met Samantha and Melissa who had arrived together. Angelique watched as Melissa sat by Dunbar's bedside and held his hand. She appeared to be very upset that he was unwell and in hospital. Angelique could not help but think that her behaviour was very strange indeed. When cross-examined by defence counsel during the trial, she denied a suggestion that she had shouted at Melissa and threatened her in the hospital. She would not be made to appear like a woman who was jealous of a child's relationship with the man with whom she had been involved.

Around the start of September, Dunbar was discharged and he visited Angelique at her flat. They were enjoying a pleasant evening when he received a phone call. Angelique heard a female voice shouting at the other end of the phone. Dunbar said, 'I'm coming, I'm coming', and immediately got up to leave. He asked to borrow Angelique's car but she refused and he took his own. He later returned to her flat and explained that he had had to perform an exorcism on Melissa. He told Angelique that Melissa had been distressed and was making noises similar to those made by a girl in the film *The Grudge*—the 2004 horror film that had starred Sarah Michelle Gellar, who is famous for playing Buffy the Vampire Slayer in a popular teenage television show. In *The Grudge*, an American nurse moved to Tokyo where she encountered a murderous supernatural force that possessed people. Dunbar said that there had been something inside Melissa and he had had to take it out.

On a later occasion in September, Dunbar arrived at Angelique's flat with his daughter, Shirley, and Angelique took the opportunity to bring up the subject of Melissa. She couldn't understand why he was still involved with the girl as Melissa needed help that he could not provide. By this stage, Melissa was officially in the care of the Health Service Executive but Angelique was not aware of this. Jill had told her that Melissa was still in Dunbar's house. Shirley was also concerned about the situation and agreed with Angelique when she told Dunbar that matters could not continue as they were. The women asked Dunbar why he still had Melissa in his house. According to Angelique, Shirley told her father that he was going to get into serious trouble over Melissa and might end up going to prison.

In her evidence to the Central Criminal Court, Angelique said that Dunbar then stated, 'I won't go to prison for her. I'll kill her. I'll strangle her. Isn't that right, Shirley?' By Angelique's account, he already had Melissa's death planned. She told the court, 'I was freaked out. I wanted nothing to do with any of them.'

Angelique had to disentangle herself from Dunbar and from Jill who had become very attached to her and was spending a great deal of time in her home, including overnight stays. The next time Jill arrived at the flat, Angelique sent her home to her father. Jill was persistent, however, and returned. In the meantime, Dunbar rang Angelique to complain that she had sent his daughter home. Angelique could not help but feel sorry for Jill so relented and let her stay. Later, she drove her back to Rathbraughan Park. 'I lied to her and said I would pick her up again but I had no intention.'

Angelique told the court that her relationship with Dunbar had lasted for five or six weeks and ended during the first week of September. In the beginning, she had spent time with him nearly every day and he had stayed the night at her house on four or five occasions during the course of the brief relationship. Angelique also said that, during the relationship, he was always on the phone to Melissa.

In September 2006, a friend of Angelique's agreed to take Dunbar's belongings from Angelique's flat back to his house. He had left blow-up beds, sleeping bags, CDs and books and had been texting Angelique demanding their return. The relationship was over.

Angelique spoke in court about her knowledge of Dunbar's history in the United Kingdom. He had told her that his name had been changed to McManus under the witness protection programme because he had given evidence against drug dealers after he and Shirley had been shot. Angelique said that he had told her that he had then had to get out of the witness protection programme because he had been threatened. Dunbar told her he had made recordings to prove that he needed to be moved and he had played them for her. She also told the court that Dunbar had told her that he had been called a pervert.

She was asked by Mr Grehan if she had discussed with Dunbar the possibility of fostering Melissa and she said she had not. Dunbar had said something to her about looking after the girl but she had not considered it seriously.

Mr Grehan then asked Angelique the glaringly obvious question. If she had been privy to and believed the threat that she said Dunbar had made on Melissa's life, why had she not reported him to gardaí? She replied that she had been scared, that it was all too much for her and that she had her own child to look after. She had felt that Dunbar was close to social workers and, quite frankly, she could not quite believe what was going on. 'I couldn't help any of them,' she said.

Angelique knew that Melissa had been missing from 14 September 2006 but did not make a statement to gardaí until April 2008, after Dunbar had been arrested and charged. She told Mr Grehan that she had talked to Garda Pat Conway on the evening when she had last dropped Jill back to Rathbraughan Park, but she had not given Garda Conway any specific information. 'I didn't believe it. I didn't want to believe it. I didn't think he would.' She said she had asked gardaí to keep what she did tell them confidential as she was terrified of Dunbar.

Mr Grehan told Angelique that Shirley Dunbar had no recollection of the conversation in which Angelique alleged Dunbar had threatened to kill Melissa. Mr Grehan suggested to Angelique that she had made up the threat. Angelique denied the suggestion and said she was only sorry that she had not come forward at an earlier stage. 'Maybe this never would have happened.'

During his cross-examination of Shirley, Mr Grehan asked her about the alleged conversation. Shirley said she had known Angelique and had been in her flat on a number of occasions, possibly five times in the company of her father. Shirley remembered that they had spoken about the possibility of her father going to prison but she said that she did not remember the exact words that had been used. She remembered that she had made him aware of the fact that he would be in serious trouble if he was found to be in breach of the court order prohibiting him from having contact with Melissa without the permission of the Health Service Executive. Mr Grehan asked Shirley if her father had said that he would strangle and kill Melissa before he would go to jail for her—would she remember him making such a threat?

'Yes,' she replied, 'but I can't say it didn't happen. I'm saying I can't remember.'

She agreed that it was a 'very striking thing to say' and she said she would have remembered it if it had happened. 'If it happened in my presence I'd say I'd remember it. I'm not saying it didn't happen.'

Angelique agreed with Mr Grehan that her relationship with Dunbar had ended badly. She said she had received hate mail and vicious text messages from him. Mr Grehan tried to paint Angelique as an unreliable lush. He put it to her that the real reason her relationship with Dunbar had ended was because she had got Jill drunk, which had infuriated Dunbar. Angelique said that such a suggestion was absolutely untrue. She also vehemently denied that her own drinking had caused the relationship to break down. She kept her cool in the witness box as the accusations about her relationship with alcohol were made, and then dismissed them quite convincingly.

Angelique said that Garda Pat Conway and Garda Colm Nevin had visited her on one occasion at her place of work. She had earlier been to see Garda Conway at the garda station. She had told them that she had concerns for Melissa's welfare and mentioned that the Dunbar girls had been fed stories about demons and devils.

Later, during his evidence, Garda Conway told the court that Angelique had come to see him at Sligo Garda Station in the middle of September 2006. She had told him that it was she who had brought Melissa to the meeting with Catherine Farrelly at Slish Wood on 24 August. Garda Conway said that Angelique had been very concerned for Melissa and revealed that the girl had been at the Dunbar house in August on the occasions when Garda Conway had called to speak to Dunbar about the teenager's whereabouts. However, from what Angelique had said to him, he did not believe that there had been an inappropriate relationship of a sexual nature between Dunbar and Melissa. He thought that any concerns about abuse suffered by Melissa were in relation to her own family. He said that Angelique had talked about Melissa's notion that she was the reincarnation of Cleopatra and that Dunbar could fight demons, but Garda Conway said he did not think it was anything serious at the time.

While being questioned by Mr Grehan, Angelique blurted out that Jill had told her that Melissa had been pregnant and that Dunbar was the father. This was hearsay evidence. A witness cannot usually repeat information they have been given by someone else. Knowing this evidence to be inadmissible, Mr Gillane for the prosecution had not questioned Angelique about the subject during his direct examination of her. When it slipped out in cross-examination, heads snapped to attention amongst the reporters. Did she just say Melissa was pregnant? Mr Grehan could not ignore the statement.

'Why,' asked defence counsel, 'if she had such explosive information about Ronnie Dunbar and a 14-year-old girl, had she not done something with it? Why not go immediately to gardaí with what she had heard?'

Angelique said she told the gardaí 'bits and pieces'. She was in shock. One minute she had been involved with a normal boyfriend and the next, he was a demon fighter.

'I didn't know what to say or what to do. The best I could say was that I had concerns about the children and about what was going on. I couldn't believe what I was hearing,' she said.

Mr Grehan put it to Angelique that she had given very

dramatic evidence that there had been a plan to strangle and kill Melissa rather than go to prison over her, and now she was saying that Melissa was three months pregnant. Again, eyebrows were raised around courtroom number two. Angelique had not specified that Melissa was three months pregnant. That must be in someone's statement in the book of evidence. There must be something to it.

Another witness in the trial later gave evidence that supported the pregnancy claim. Sarah (who also gave evidence in relation to Danny Mills) said that she lived near Lis na nÓg and had got to know Melissa Mahon in August 2006. She also knew the Dunbars and was friendly with Samantha and Jill. At the time, Sarah was going out with a teenage boy who was resident at Lis na nÓg. Sarah had been with Melissa and another teenage girl in Sligo town on the day that Melissa had bought a pregnancy test in Tesco. They had gone to the toilets of McDonald's and Melissa had taken the test. Sarah said that she saw the stick and that it had been positive.

She said, 'Melissa was kinda happy, kinda delighted in a way.'

Sarah did not say so in court, but her pre-trial statements to gardaí indicated that she believed that Dunbar was having sex with Melissa and that he was the father of her baby.

The other teenage girl who was in the toilets with Melissa and Sarah for the test (who also cannot be named because of her age) gave evidence. She agreed with Sarah and said that, she too, had seen the test and that it had been positive.

Mr Grehan suggested to Angelique that all she had told gardaí in confidence was that she had driven Melissa to the meeting with Catherine Farrelly in Slish Wood and had been directed to do so by Dunbar. Mr Grehan suggested that she had confessed to her involvement in that meeting only to cover herself. Angelique disagreed and told the jury that when she had agreed to bring Melissa to the meeting, surreptitiously or not, she had believed that she was doing a good deed.

Surely, according to Mr Grehan, if Dunbar had really made the threat to kill Melissa it would have surfaced long before Angelique's statement of April 2008. There was no answer to that.

10 RUTH NOONEY

On the 18th day of the trial, another of Dunbar's girlfriends was called to give evidence for the prosecution. It was Friday afternoon and the court had been listening to a string of DNA experts give technical evidence about the painstaking process that had been undertaken to prove the identity of the remains found at Lough Gill. The Mahon family had, as they had done for any evidence relating to the remains, absented themselves from the court. In the afternoon, a fragile lady in her twenties, though looking older, took the stand. She seemed nervous and there was talk among reporters that she may have been under some form of sedation.

Ruth Nooney was born and raised in Sligo in the early 1980s. She lived in Galway for some time but returned to Sligo in July 2007. She stayed in a bed and breakfast with her son for a week when she first came back and then, on 18 July 2007, rented a three-bedroom terraced house in Rathbraughan Park.

A couple of days after she moved into the estate, her younger brother, who was 11 years old, came to visit her. He was very fond of water and there was a stream at the end of her street so he went outside to take a look. Ruth followed her brother and found him talking to Ronnie Dunbar. She chatted briefly with him and then continued on her way.

A few days later, Ruth was having a problem getting her television to work. She saw Danny Lynnott, Shirley Dunbar's boyfriend, passing by on the street and called to him. Danny did not know how to fix the television, but he knew a man who did. He fetched Dunbar from his house three doors down. Dunbar arrived at Ruth's house with Jill at his hip. Ruth had met the girl before, down by the stream when she had chatted to Dunbar. Shirley Dunbar came into the house looking for her boyfriend and they left Dunbar and Jill in Ruth's house where they stayed for the evening and spent the night.

Ronnie fixed the channels and then the three of them settled down to watch DVDs. With Jill asleep in a chair, Ruth sat up all night talking to Dunbar. Father and daughter left the following morning, but they returned the next day and stayed that night as well. A relationship quickly developed between Dunbar and Ruth. Romance blossomed on the third night that he stayed. From then on, Dunbar spent most nights in her house. He would return to his own home in the mornings to look after his beloved dogs. Ruth started accompanying him to the gym and they would go for walks together in Slish Wood. In the beginning, they got along extremely well.

Ruth told the court that Dunbar did not drink alcohol and didn't agree with her drinking. They had a row over it and she stopped going out to socialise. Jill did not go to school and would spend her time in Ruth's house with her father. Jill would stay at Ruth's house even when Dunbar was not there and, eventually, Ruth converted a bedroom for her.

At the start of their relationship, Ruth and Dunbar would go for walks every day. Ruth said Dunbar enjoyed being active, loved the outdoors and hated living in the town. They would drive to Slish Wood in his black BMW—this was after the days of spins in the little blue Fiat. He would drive out past Parkes Castle and stop at the car park over looking Lough Gill. The first time this happened, Dunbar got out of the car, walked to the front and stood for several minutes taking in the view. Ruth sat in the passenger seat and smoked a cigarette. Dunbar said nothing and got back into the car to drive to Slish Wood. They went to Slish

Wood every day but Ronnie stopped to examine the lake only twice. He told Ruth that his ancestors had had something to do with the castle. At Slish Wood, they would walk along a trail and take time to sit down along the way and talk. Jill accompanied them on their walks only once and would usually stay at home to babysit Ruth's son. On one occasion, Dunbar stopped at Lidl to buy a blow-up rubber dinghy.

Ruth told the court that her relationship with Dunbar had come to an end in late 2007, although information would emerge following her court appearance that contradicted this assertion.

The court had already heard that Melissa and the Dunbar girls had strange notions about Dunbar and his demon-fighting abilities. Ruth expanded on that topic. She said that Dunbar had his beliefs and she had hers. It was not entirely clear from the way she phrased that sentence whether she meant that she had her own separate and different beliefs or that she shared and agreed with his. Reporters gave her the benefit of the doubt in that day's court coverage but, later, she would explain herself more clearly to the media.

She told the court that Ronnie believed that a new world order was coming and, when that day came, he would be king. When it all 'kicked off', he would be king of the battlefield. His obsessive gym routine would keep him fit for that day and his precious pit bulls would be at his side during the fight. Ever the master manipulator, he had told Ruth that he would only be able to take with him the people he could trust. Looks were exchanged among observers in courtroom number two. In this most tragic of cases, this evidence seemed almost comical.

As their relationship deepened, Dunbar knew he would have to address the issue of Melissa Mahon. There had been talk in the town and Ruth was bound to hear rumour and gossip. It was early August 2007 and approaching the one-year anniversary of Melissa's disappearance and Dunbar knew that interest in the case would be reignited.

He went to Ruth's house and told her that he had something to explain. He said that a little girl had gone missing the year earlier and it would be on the news again. He told her she would hear rumours that he had been going out with the girl, but, of course, he had not, she was so young, she was a 14-year-old girl. Dunbar said the girl's father had been abusing her and he had stepped in to get her help and to get her into care. The girl would often call to his house and she was good friends with his daughters. He told Ruth that he had been helping gardaí and he was the only one who had done anything to help the girl, so, naturally enough, she had run to him when she was upset.

Ruth told the court that Dunbar had played her recordings of conversations he had had with gardaí and had shown her articles that had been published about Melissa in the *Sligo Weekender*. He had told her that he had kept the recordings to use as evidence if, and when, he was made a scapegoat for Melissa's disappearance. Ruth said she had heard a recorded conversation between Garda Pat Conway and Dunbar in which Dunbar had expressed his concern that he would be blamed. Dunbar had told Garda Conway that he had heard all sorts of rumours that Melissa was here, there and everywhere. He had heard that she had been spotted in England and that she was pregnant. Garda Conway had said that Melissa's mother, Mary, would not let any information out and was, in that sense, like an old IRA woman. Mary Mahon had told Garda Conway that Melissa was staying with family members in England but she would not say who those family members were or how she had come by this information.

Ruth fell deeply in love with Dunbar very quickly and he told her that he wanted to be honest with her and tell her the truth before she heard vicious and untrue rumours from anyone else.

On the way back from one of their walks, Dunbar drove Ruth around to the house in Rathbraughan Park where Melissa's parents had lived. He pointed to the house and told her that the family had moved. Ruth thought this was strange. Surely, if your daughter was missing, you would stay in the same house in case she came back. Dunbar agreed with Ruth and told her that the family was troubled and then repeated the allegation that Melissa's father had been abusing her.

After he had told Ruth about Melissa, Dunbar would often

bring the teenager up in conversation and would ask Ruth what she thought might have happened to her. Did she think the girl was missing or dead? He told her that he and Angelique Sheridan had planned to foster Melissa but he had broken up with Angelique because she had got Jill drunk. Ruth told him about a website in the United Kingdom which was dedicated to finding missing people. Dunbar told her that he would travel to England to find Melissa.

He said that Melissa had been going missing constantly before she finally disappeared and had been drinking and taking drugs with Samantha in a house with loads of boys. He told Ruth that the last time he had seen Melissa was on his birthday in September 2006. She had arrived at his house but he had refused to let her in. She had brought him a present but he told her that he did not want her around his house, so she threw his present over the back wall. He told Ruth that the last he had ever heard from Melissa was a call he had received from an old man the night she had run away from a foster family. The old man had asked Dunbar if he was the girl's father.

He told Ruth that since Melissa's disappearance, her sister had been texting him, asking how he was doing and telling him that Melissa had been seen in England.

Around the anniversary of Melissa's disappearance, Dunbar came to Ruth and told her that he had just received a phone call but all he could hear was a female with an English accent saying, 'Dad, Dad, Dad.' He thought it might have been his eldest daughter, Kirsty, but he had checked and it was not her. Then he said that it might have been Melissa.

Before Dunbar and Ruth's relationship floundered, she was summoned to see a social worker at the end of November 2007. Dunbar waited outside as she talked to a Health Service Executive employee who discussed Dunbar with her. When she came out, Dunbar questioned her about what had been said. They broke up as a result of that conversation. She told the court that she didn't even pack her belongings, she just left him.

Ruth and Dunbar had become engaged before they broke up. Under cross-examination, Ruth told Mr Grehan that she had been madly in love. When she had met Dunbar, she had come out of a very serious and very bad relationship in which she had been hurt. Ruth became visibly upset as she spoke of that relationship and Mr Grehan apologised for bringing up painful memories. She composed herself and said that Dunbar had brought her to the gym with him to build up her strength. He had brought out a better side of her and, in the beginning, that was very good for her. He had gone on and on about the new world order and had said he could only bring those who were strong with him. Trust was a big issue for him and he had accused her of having flirty eyes. He had become jealous and did not appreciate the manner in which he believed she behaved with other people.

Ruth said that she had an awful lot of trouble with Dunbar's daughters. Samantha had been unhappy about the relationship from day one. Ruth said that Samantha had tried to attack her with a pen knife and, on another occasion, had thumped her in the stomach when she was pregnant. Ruth told Mr Grehan that Samantha had threatened to kick the baby out of Ruth and had said she would break up Ruth's relationship with her father. Samantha was also accused of kicking in Ruth's front door when Ruth was not in the house. Ruth said she had reported that incident to gardaí. Shirley was also unhappy about her father's relationship with Ruth. By contrast, Jill was very nice and Ruth had got on well with her at the beginning. In each dispute with Shirley and Samantha, however, Dunbar had taken Ruth's side.

As the court day drew to a close, Ruth left the witness box clearly relieved that her ordeal was over. The jury and judge left the room and Ruth turned to Dunbar. Before officers led him back to the prison van, Ruth embraced the man she had told the jury she was no longer in a relationship with. They sat together and talked quietly in the courtroom for several minutes before it was time for Dunbar to be taken away.

The day after Dunbar was convicted, Ruth made a splash in the tabloid press. She spoke to the *Sun* newspaper about her relationship with Dunbar in which she revealed that they were still engaged and had had a son together. When she had mentioned in court that she had been pregnant she hadn't stated that Dunbar was the father.

Ronnie Dunbar pictured with his daughters in earlier years, Samantha is on the right and Shirley is in the foreground. The Sligo man won custody of the girls, after their mother left him following years of abuse. (© *Sunday World*)

Ronnie Dunbar pictured at the front door of his home at Rathbraughan Park in 2008 when *Sunday World* journalist Paul Williams confronted him about allegations made in that newspaper by Dunbar's daughter Shirley. (© *Sunday World*)

Melissa Mahon, Ronnie Dunbar's 14-year-old victim, who died in September 2006 and was dumped in the River Bonet. Her remains were found on the shore of Lough Gill in February 2008 after Dunbar's daughter Samantha came forward with information. (© *Sunday World*)

Melissa Mahon's funeral on Wednesday, 12 August 2009, following Dunbar's trial and the release of her remains from garda custody. She was buried at Sligo Cemetery after a funeral mass at St Anne's Church. Pictured are members of her family, including her sister Leeanna Mahon (far left) and her father, Frederick. It was reported that Mary Mahon did not attend her daughter's funeral. (© *Sunday World*)

Melissa Mahon's parents, Mary and Frederick, pictured leaving the Four Courts on the day Ronnie Dunbar was convicted of manslaughter. They were later criticised by the trial judge, Mr Justice Barry White, for their attitude following Melissa's disappearance. The judge called Mary's victim impact statement 'disingenuous in the extreme'. (© *Photocall*)

Angelique Sheridan, Ronnie Dunbar's former girlfriend, pictured leaving the Four Courts following her evidence for the prosecution. She told the jury that Dunbar had said that he would not go to jail over Melissa and would kill her by strangling her. (© *Collins Photo*)

Samantha Dunbar, the State's star witness against her father. The then 18-year-old gave evidence via live television link and told the jury that she saw her father on a bed with Melissa Mahon with his arm around the girl's neck, before he tied her into a sleeping bag and dumped her body in the River Bonet. (© Court Pix)

Ronnie Dunbar's daughter Shirley pictured posing for the *Sunday World*. Shirley was not present when Melissa was killed and her body dumped, but she was the person to whom Samantha finally admitted what had happened. Shirley gave a number of interviews to the *Sunday World* following her sister's revelations. (*© Sunday World*)

Ruth Nooney, another former girlfriend of Ronnie Dunbar and mother of his young son, pictured leaving the Four Courts after telling the jury that Dunbar believed in the coming of a new world order in which he would be king of the battlefield. (*© Collins Photo*)

Mr Justice Barry White, the judge who presided over the trial of Ronnie Dunbar and imposed a life sentence for Melissa Mahon's manslaughter. He said Dunbar had disposed of the girl in a manner 'not befitting an animal'. *(© Court Pix)*

She told the press that she was heartbroken over Dunbar's conviction and devastated by the prospect of him facing a long prison sentence. Their son was 11 months old when his father was convicted and Dunbar had not yet met the child. Ruth was concerned about the stigma her son would face as the child of a child killer. She told *Sun* reporter Joanne McElgunn that all she wanted was for her Ronnie to come home so they could be a family.

Ruth reportedly became pregnant with Dunbar's child in September 2007, around the time of his 43rd birthday. She was delighted, although less so when it became clear in February 2008 that Dunbar was the chief suspect in the murder of Melissa Mahon. Ruth decided to leave Dunbar because she was afraid that she ran the risk of losing her other son from a previous relationship if she stayed with him. She told the *Sun* that she had never stopped loving Dunbar.

Dunbar was already in prison facing murder charges when their child was born in July 2008. Because Ruth was to be called as a witness for the prosecution, she was not supposed to have any contact with him. Ruth told the newspaper that she instructed friends to tell Dunbar that their child had died.

While her greatest concern was the stigma that her child would suffer, she still believed that Dunbar was innocent. She saw him as a kind person who was incapable of hurting anyone. When she got over the trauma of giving birth while the father was in jail awaiting trial for murder, she changed her mind about her child's future and told an 'overjoyed' Dunbar that their son was alive.

She was crushed when Dunbar was convicted as she did not want people to think of him as a monster. He was the love of her life and she wanted to grow old with him.

Ruth told the press that she did not believe that Dunbar had ever had sex with Melissa Mahon. She did not think from her intimate knowledge of him that he would be interested in a young girl. He was loving and gentle and she would have been able to spot any 'evil' in him. His interest in Melissa had been fatherly. He had wanted to protect her.

Ruth was a broken person when she met Dunbar, having

suffered in past relationships. She believed that he had fixed her and brought back the old Ruth. She vowed to fight to have his name cleared and implored readers not to judge the man by his appearance. He was a lovely man. She believed the truth had not yet been revealed.

When she arrived at the Central Criminal Court to give her testimony for the prosecution, it was the first time she had seen Dunbar since December 2007. All of her old feelings had come flooding back. She visited him in prison the next day and showed him photographs of their son. She vowed to wait for him for as long as it took.

However, Dunbar had other ideas. The following day, it was reported in the same newspaper that he had refused to maintain contact with Ruth. He said he loved her but, following his conviction, said she should forget him and get on with her life without him. He had decided to refuse visits, telephone calls or letters from her. Ruth was determined to keep the relationship alive and rang prison officials to pass on messages of love and support to the convicted killer. She told the *Sun* that she feared he would kill himself in prison. He hated being cooped up and lived for the outdoors. He had dreamed of living in the countryside, so being locked up was a special kind of punishment for him.

Another newspaper had reported that Ruth intended to marry Dunbar in prison but she denied that there was any truth to that story. She said Dunbar would not agree to it. He was a romantic and would want their big day to be special.

By the end of June, newspaper reports suggested that Ruth had had a change of heart and had decided to end the love affair herself in a phone call to Castlerea Prison. She was quoted in the *News of the World* as saying, 'Ronnie is on his own now. I just can't do this anymore. It's over. I'm wiping my hands of the whole situation and moving on.'

Earlier that month, it had been reported that Ruth feared that she and her children would be attacked by vigilantes because of her relationship with Dunbar. She said, 'I am a total outcast now and a prisoner in my own home but the only crime I committed was to fall in love.'

11 | **THE STAR WITNESS**

S amantha Louise Conroy was born to Ronnie Dunbar and Lisa Conroy in the United Kingdom on 29 March 1991.

In her father's trial, she was the prosecution's star witness. Having kept the terrible secret for over 16 months, it was she who finally cracked and told gardaí what had happened to Melissa. Her time in the witness box came on the eighth day of the trial, 30 April 2009.

The general rule is for a witness to be present in the courtroom to give oral evidence and be cross-examined by defence lawyers. Section 13 of the Criminal Evidence Act 1992, however, allows a witness to give evidence by live television link if the person is under 18 years of age. If the witness is older, he or she may give evidence by this mechanism with the permission of the court. The prosecution called several witnesses who fell into the first category, including teenagers who knew Melissa, and Jill, who was 16 years old at the time of the trial. Birth certificates were furnished to the court in relation to those witnesses and Mr Justice White was, therefore, satisfied that they should give their evidence by television link.

Samantha turned 18 before the trial, but the prosecution argued that she was a vulnerable witness and successfully applied to the trial judge to allow her to give her evidence by television link. The concern was that Samantha's emotional state would impact on her ability to give her evidence coherently. The State called a medical witness and Samantha's current social worker who both told the court that they believed that Samantha might not be able to cope and could freeze in the witness box, rendering her unable to testify. The court heard that she was suffering symptoms of post-traumatic stress disorder. Mr Grehan indicated that his client would be prepared to stay in the holding cell while his daughter was on the stand, but that offer was rejected by the judge.

Mr Justice White said that the law had created a certain presumption that may or may not truly reflect reality. The 1992 act presumed an overnight change in a witness on their 18th birthday. He said Samantha had only recently turned 18 and he was satisfied that she was a vulnerable person and that there existed bona fide health concerns. Testifying in open court could potentially have a detrimental effect on her that could create a real risk to her health and welfare.

The trial had been sitting at courtroom number two in the Round Hall of the Four Courts but had to move to courtroom sixteen on the second floor of the building to avail of television-link facilities. The situation was not ideal. Courtroom sixteen is unsuitable in terms of space and lacks a proper room to which the judge can retire in the event that the court has to rise for a short time. The jury room is cramped and the seating for the public and press is severely limited. The Dunbar trial spent five days in courtroom sixteen listening to witnesses via television link. The bench along the back of the room was always full, leaving reporters, gardaí and observers standing in a huddle by the door. Dunbar had been sitting on the back bench near the door and his view of the television screens was blocked by those forced to stand, so he had to be moved into the witness box while the teenagers gave their evidence.

Samantha appeared on screen dressed in a white shirt and with her dark hair cut into a bob with a straight fringe. She had a strong English accent and spoke firmly and clearly. Gardaí had told reporters that the Dunbar girls were deeply damaged individuals and perhaps a more timid character was expected than the assured girl who appeared. She told Ms Kennedy that she had been born in England and had lived there until she was 12. She was then moved to Scotland and had arrived in Sligo in August 2005. She had lived with various aunts in Sligo with her younger sister, Jill, her older sister, Shirley, and her father before a house became available in the Rathbraughan Estate in September 2005. Shortly after her birthday in March 2006, Samantha started at Youth Reach in Sligo, the State-run training and education programme for early school leavers who require a 'second chance' to acquire an education. There, she did woodwork and cooking and physical education. She had started third year at the Mercy College in September 2005 and had been due to sit her Junior Certificate exams the following spring but her attendance had been poor and so she had ended up at Youth Reach.

During 2005, her sisters, Shirley and Jill, had also been at Mercy College and they had all made a number of friends. Jill made friends with the Mahon girls, Melissa and Leeanna. Melissa and Jill were both in first year and Samantha said that, initially, she hadn't liked Melissa because she had got her sister into trouble. She had changed her mind, however, when Melissa had started to skip school with them. 'I got to like her then,' she said. The two Mahon girls plus Samantha and Jill continued to miss classes and were eventually suspended by the head nun at the school.

The Mahon family had lived at Garavogue Villas when Samantha had first met her new friends, but they had then moved to the Rathbraughan Estate. The Dunbars were in number 64 and the Mahons moved into number 68. Samantha said that she if she looked out of the back windows of her own home, she could see the Mahon house. Leeanna and Melissa had begun to visit the Dunbar house every other night. They would watch a DVD and eat dinner with Samantha, her sisters and her father. Samantha said that Melissa had begun to run away from home and ran to her father in August 2006. She said that Melissa had stayed the night in her house and had slept downstairs with her father.

The Dunbar house comprised a sitting room, kitchen, back garden and shed on the ground floor and three bedrooms upstairs. The large bedroom overlooking the front of the house was occupied by her father, the other two bedrooms were at the back of the house—one contained two single beds which were used by Samantha and Jill.

Samantha said that during one of Melissa's disappearances that summer, she had had a conversation with her in the sitting room of the house that her father had overheard. Melissa had told Samantha that she had fallen in love with Dunbar and was having a sexual relationship with him. The girls had been sitting together on the sofa when Melissa had made her confession. Melissa had told Samantha that she had first had sex with her father on the night she had run away from home and had slept downstairs with Dunbar. Samantha told the court that her father had then walked into the room and admitted that what Melissa had said was true.

She recalled Garda Pat Conway calling to her house with social worker, Catherine Farrelly, and said that her father had seen them through the window and had told Melissa to hide behind the sofa. Dunbar had then told the visitors that he did not know where Melissa was and would ring his connections to see if she could be found.

Samantha told Ms Kennedy that she remembered staying at Angelique Sheridan's house with her father, Jill and Melissa. Dunbar had slept upstairs with his girlfriend and the teenagers had stayed on a blow-up bed in the sitting room. They had gone to Angelique's flat to enable Dunbar to carry out his plan for Melissa to meet up with her social worker. Samantha said that Melissa had gone to a phonebox in Dromahair with Dunbar and had telephoned Catherine Farrelly to arrange a meeting in Slish Wood. The following morning, she had been in Angelique's sitting room with Melissa and her father when Dunbar had rung Catherine Farrelly and told her that he would meet her at Markievicz House. He had then told the social worker that he did not at that stage know Melissa's whereabouts. Samantha said she had travelled in her father's car with him to pick up Catherine and had sat in the back seat as he had driven to Slish Wood. She had known that Melissa would be travelling to the meeting area in the boot of Angelique's car and that Angelique and Jill would hide in the woods and leave Melissa on a bench, just as her father had planned.

Samantha said it had taken around 20 minutes to drive to Slish Wood and, when they had arrived, they had seen Melissa sitting alone at the picnic bench in a clearing in the wood. Dunbar had hugged Melissa and then Samantha, as she had been earlier instructed to do by her father, had hugged her friend as though she had not seen her in years.

Samantha continued with her evidence, saying that she and her father had sat beside Melissa and Catherine Farrelly had taken the seat opposite. As Catherine had talked to Melissa, Dunbar had got up and walked away but he was never too far from them. Melissa had refused to tell Catherine where she was living and there was a conversation about money that resulted in Dunbar handing Melissa cash that Catherine said he would be reimbursed for. When the meeting had ended, Samantha had got back into her father's car with Catherine. They had then returned to Markievicz House where Catherine had given Dunbar money to reimburse him for the cash he had given Melissa. Then, he and Samantha had driven to Angelique's flat where Melissa, Jill and Angelique had been waiting for them in the sitting room. Samantha had sat down beside Melissa and listened as her father, having taken a seat opposite, had begun to try to persuade Melissa to go into residential care. Melissa had been initially reluctant but had eventually given in. Samantha said Melissa had not been happy about the decision but had gone along with what Dunbar had wanted. He had told Melissa that she should go into care because that would enable him and Angelique to fight to get her out and look after her themselves.

Samantha told the court that Melissa had packed up the small number of clothes she had had in Rathbraughan Park and had gone with Dunbar to Lis na nÓg. Samantha, as usual, had accompanied them. There, Melissa and Samantha had been introduced to staff and other residents. Dunbar had left both girls there for the day and had returned at 10 p.m. to collect his daughter. Samantha became a regular visitor to Lis na nÓg to see Melissa.

During this time, Jill was spending a great deal of her time at Angelique's house and often slept there.

Samantha continued her evidence saying that not long after Melissa had gone into care, Dunbar needed to go into hospital for an operation. Melissa had been upset when she found out. On the day of his operation, Melissa and Angelique had both arrived at the hospital but, according to Samantha, they had fought and Melissa had run away. She was found sitting on the floor outside the operating theatre waiting for Dunbar. That night, she had gone back to the Dunbar house with Samantha and they had had a party with some teenage friends. Two girls and a boy had stayed in the house with Samantha and Melissa but Dunbar found out about it and quizzed his daughter the next day.

When Dunbar had left the hospital, he had taken Melissa back to Lis na nÓg. The teenage boy, who had been in Dunbar's house the previous evening, had been sitting on the wall outside the home. Samantha said that the boy had told her father that he had slept with Melissa and Dunbar had reacted by grabbing the teenager from the wall. According to Samantha, the boy had then threatened to shoot Dunbar, which sent the older man into a rage. Samantha said she thought that Melissa had stayed in Lis na nÓg that evening and Dunbar had returned to the hospital.

When he was discharged again, he had driven Melissa and Samantha to Hazel Wood, a forested area at the side of Lough Gill. They had been supposed to go for a walk but Melissa had wanted to go back to the Dunbar house. He had refused to take her there and she had run off into the woods. Samantha had told her father that Melissa had a lighter so he had told her to follow her friend. Samantha told the court that, at this stage, she and Melissa had become best friends. Dunbar had not been able follow Melissa himself because he had not been able to walk comfortably after his operation. Samantha said that she had found Melissa lying on the ground in the woods sniffing gas from the lighter. A garda had appeared and Melissa had jumped up and started to run, but he had caught up with her quickly. The girls had been brought back to Dunbar and he had taken Melissa back to the care home later that night.

Samantha then gave evidence about what had happened on 13 September 2006. She said that she had been walking home from Youth Reach with friends when she had seen Melissa outside Lis na nÓg. The gardaí had been there and Melissa had been screaming and kicking. Samantha had then seen Melissa make a bolt for it and run down the road but the garda had caught her and put her into a patrol car. The following morning, Dunbar had told Samantha that he had received a telephone call in the middle of the night from an old man who had drugged Melissa and had then rung Dunbar to ask him to come and get her. Dunbar told her that he had refused to go. Samantha knew that her father had received a text message from Melissa saying that she was with her social worker and was safe.

By this time, the Dunbars had moved to 63 Rathbraughan Park. Samantha told the court that when she had been living at number 63, and after Melissa had been taken away by gardaí, she had seen the curtains moving in the box bedroom of number 64. She had asked her father if Melissa was there and he had confirmed that she was. Dunbar had told Samantha to cook for Melissa and to bring the food over to her. She was to climb over the back wall to get into their former home. He told Samantha that he had found Melissa in the garden of number 64 and that she had been crying and had had slashes on her arms. Melissa had not known that the Dunbars had moved. She had been trying to get into number 64 thinking that they were still there. Dunbar had given Melissa the key to number 64. Samantha said her father had had the front and back door keys cut for that house before they had moved out and had returned the original keys to the letting agent. Her father had also cut a hole in the bottom of a bed in number 64 to hide Melissa when the gardaí came to the house. He had then done the same to a bed in number 63.

Samantha said that, the next morning, she and Jill had been at home but that their father had been missing from the house and had not been answering his phone. She had known where he was —in number 64 with Melissa.

That evening, Samantha had cooked dinner for Melissa and had asked her father if Melissa could come over to number 63 to eat with them. She said that Jill had spent that evening with Angelique Sheridan. Dunbar had said that Melissa could come over so Samantha said that she had climbed over the back wall and had gone into the house. Samantha had begged her father to let Melissa stay in the new house for the night and he had agreed. Melissa had been wearing a pink hooded top, white trainers and black tracksuit bottoms. She had asked Samantha for a nightdress and was given an old one that no longer fitted Samantha. It was short and yellow with puffy sleeves and a frill along the bottom. It had a Beauty and the Beast design on the front and had belonged to Samantha when she had been 10 years old. The nightdress was a bit big for Melissa's slight frame, but would do. Melissa had kept her tracksuit bottoms on underneath the nightdress and had been wearing stripy socks.

Samantha said that the next morning had been a Thursday, she didn't know the date, but knew it was mid-September. She thought it was a couple of days after Melissa had been taken to the foster family by the Health Service Executive. When Samantha had got up at 8 a.m. to go to Youth Reach, she had walked out of her bedroom and had seen Melissa wearing the same clothes as the night before—she had been standing in the back bedroom looking out the window, watching Dunbar in the garden. Samantha had gone into the room and given her friend a hug and a kiss goodbye.

Youth Reach had finished for the day at 4.30 p.m. and it had taken Samantha half an hour to walk home. She had arrived at 63 Rathbraughan Park at 5 p.m. Samantha said she had been in good humour and let herself into the house but the first thing she had seen was Jill crying as she smoked a cigarette in the sitting room.

Samantha told the court that Jill had told her not to go upstairs, so she had done the opposite. She had climbed the stairs and had gone into her father's bedroom. The curtains had been closed and the room had been dark but she had been able to see Melissa and her father lying on the bed. They were fully clothed and lying on top of the covers, each on their left side with Dunbar lying behind Melissa. He had had his arm around Melissa's neck and Samantha had thought he was giving her a hug. She had then walked out of the room. Jill had been standing behind her, still crying. Samantha said she had thought her father and Melissa were getting up to something sexual and so she had burst back into the bedroom. Melissa had still been on her side, she hadn't moved. Samantha said she had turned on the bedroom light and her father had jumped off the bed. Melissa had then fallen on to her back as Dunbar had moved away from her. Melissa's eyes had been closed, her face had been purple and her lips blue. Samantha said her father had left the room and she had got on top of Melissa and had tried to resuscitate her. She had thought Melissa was trying to breathe and she had been able to see her friend's chest moving up and down. Samantha said Melissa had been struggling for air and a high-pitched noise had been coming from her mouth.

'I was screaming her name. She didn't respond. She wasn't moving, she was just trying to breathe.'

Samantha told the court that she had sat on Melissa's legs and had pushed down on her chest. She said she had been trying to save Melissa's life but the girl was not breathing anymore. She was dead. During all this, Jill had been in the corner of the room, still crying.

Melissa was still wearing the same clothes, the Beauty and the Beast nightdress, black tracksuit bottoms and socks. Her hair had been dyed black and tied back. Samantha said Dunbar had cut Melissa's fringe into a Cleopatra style.

Samantha told the court that, by this stage, she had also been in tears and had heard her father coming back upstairs. She and Jill had run to each other as he had come back into the bedroom with a greyish-blue-coloured sleeping bag in his hands. She said he had taken Melissa off the bed and had put her, head first, into the sleeping bag and had zipped it up. He had then gone to his wardrobe, taken out a blue tie and had used it to tie up the end of the bag at Melissa's feet. Samantha told the court that she had noticed a strong smell of urine coming from the sleeping bag.

Dunbar had lifted the sleeping bag roughly and had carried

Melissa like a rag doll to the bottom of the stairs. He had looked out the front door to check if anyone was around, left Melissa on the floor and had then got into his car to reverse it back to the door. Samantha and Jill had watched him from the house. He had opened the car's boot, lifted Melissa's body and tried to put her into the boot. Samantha said the body hadn't fitted, so he had tried to shove her into the space. Samantha said she had heard a snapping sound, which she took to be Melissa's neck breaking before her father succeeded in forcing the body into the car.

It had been around 5.30 p.m. and was still bright outside. Dunbar had ordered his daughters into the car as he shut the boot.

Samantha said she had been frightened and had done what she was told. She had got into the back of the car and her sister had sat in the front passenger seat. Samantha said that Dunbar had not shown any emotion. He had got into the car and driven 20 minutes to a spot along the River Bonet. He had taken the girls to that location before when he had called it the 'secret wood' because it was in the middle of nowhere and no one knew about it. At the time of that first visit, there had been a barge on the river that had been tied by a blue rope to a tree and Dunbar had talked to his daughters about renovating it and living there. This time, when they reached the 'secret wood', Dunbar had continued to drive for a further five minutes along a rough and bumpy path. Samantha remembered the location well and, later, was able to show the exact spot to Detective Sergeant Con Lee in the company of her sister, Shirley, and a social worker.

On the evening Melissa had died, Dunbar had parked the car and he and the girls had got out. He had opened the boot, lifted Melissa out and put her on the ground. He had then closed the boot and gone to look for stones that he put into his pockets. He had then gone back to Melissa's body and lifted the sleeping bag with one hand by the end he had tied with the neck tie. He had then dragged the bag along a winding path to the end of the wooded area until he had reached the grass that led down to the edge of the river.

Samantha told the court that the ground was muddy and

bumpy and that she and her sister had walked behind their father as he had dragged Melissa's body. At the edge of the river, he had told Samantha to grab the end of the sleeping bag where the tie was. She told the court that she did so because he had told her to.

'My dad was a very controlling man and we were scared of him,' she said. 'He was a built man and we were only young girls at the time.'

Dunbar had told her to walk into the water and so she had ended up knee high in the river. He had got in up to his thighs and then told Samantha to swing the bag and throw it into the water on the count of three. The bag had gone into the river but was lower down in the water on her father's side because he was stronger. The bag had flooded with water and had slowly started to sink. Dunbar had then taken the stones he had collected earlier and had thrown them at the bag. He had told his daughters that if it did not sink he would have to jump in after it. They had waited another five minutes to make sure Melissa had disappeared. Samantha said she had noticed that the current of the river had been running quickly at the time.

Samantha said that, as they had walked back to the car, Dunbar had told his daughters that they had been accessories to their friend's murder and he would do the same to them as he had done to her if they went to the gardaí or told anyone else about what they had done. Samantha told the court that he had repeated the threat over and over again, scaring her and her sister, as they drove home to Rathbraughan Park.

Samantha had been terrified. 'My father was a very dominant man. Everyone was afraid of him because he was so aggressive.'

She said she knew the route her father had taken to the River Bonet well. Dunbar had taken them for spins out in that direction and they had gone for walks with the dogs in the area. She said she had not gone back to that place until February 2008 when she had indicated to gardaí where Melissa's body had been dumped.

Ms Kennedy sent a garda into the room from which Samantha was giving her evidence to ask her if she could identify exhibits in the case. She was shown the sleeping bag, the nightdress and the neck tie that gardaí had recovered at Lough Gill. Samantha confirmed that they were the same items that Melissa had been wearing and had been wrapped in when she had been thrown into the water. Samantha was also shown photographs of the location where the body had been found and of the bed she had said she had seen her father lying on with Melissa. She was shown a photograph of a hole cut into the base of the bed and said that was where her father had made a hiding place for Melissa so that gardaí would not know she was in the house if they came to look for her.

Samantha said that after Dunbar was satisfied that Melissa's body had disappeared under the water, they had got back into the little blue car and had taken the same route home. Samantha thought it was around 7.30 p.m. when they had returned to the house. Dunbar had football practice three times a week and, on a Thursday evening, he played in Collooney. That evening, one of the men he trained with had arrived at the house to drive Dunbar and his daughters to the Teeling Sports Centre. The girls usually accompanied their father to the practices, and that night was no different. The session had lasted for around an hour. Samantha said that, that evening, Dunbar had laughed and had behaved normally with his friends as they had played.

When they had returned home, she had gone straight to bed, tired and upset. The next morning she had not been able to face going to Youth Reach and when she had got out of bed, she had found her father cleaning out the car. A teenage girl from across the street had been helping him. Dunbar had removed the car seat covers and burned them in the fireplace in the living room of their house.

Samantha said Melissa had travelled in the boot of the car on a number of occasions when they had gone for drives around the countryside. When she had been 'on the run' during the summer of 2006, Melissa would climb into the boot with a pillow and Dunbar would put a blanket over her to hide her. As soon as they got out of Sligo, Melissa would climb into the back seat and sit beside Samantha.

The day after Melissa had died, Dunbar had scrubbed his car with disinfectant. He had cleaned his bedroom, stripped the bed and disinfected the mattress. He had put the bed linen in the washing machine and bleached his bed's wooden frame. Some clothes belonging to Melissa were still in the house, hooded tops, tracksuit bottoms, underwear and runners. He had put all of those items into the fire. He had also burned a photograph of him wearing the tie that he had used to tie up the sleeping bag in which he had dumped Melissa. He did not usually wear ties but had put one on the previous Christmas and someone had taken a picture of the unusual event.

'He used white spirit to make the fire burn even more,' said Samantha. 'He said he was getting rid of all traces of Melissa.'

There had been three similar sleeping bags in the house that had been used for camping trips. Dunbar had bought them before Melissa had first run away from her own home. Melissa had been tied into one and Dunbar had burned a second one in the fire that day. Samantha told the court that, the following day, her father had driven her and Jill out to another spot along the river. He had taken the third sleeping bag and walked into the water. He had then unzipped the bag, opened it up and placed a rock on top of it to see how well it would sink.

Having told the court about what had happened in September 2006, Samantha was questioned about the events of January 2008. She had been staying with her sister, Shirley, at 69 Rathbraughan Park for two weeks when, on the last day of the month, she had had an argument with her mother on the phone. Samantha had spent the preceding Christmas with her mother, Lisa Conroy, in the United Kingdom. Samantha said that, following the row, and after a conversation with Shirley, the gardaí had been called and she had made a statement.

Mr Grehan then began his cross-examination of the State's key witness. Samantha's evidence had been damning and convincing. Mr Grehan asked her if she realised how important her evidence was in this trial and pointed out that a lot of what she had described in detail was based on what she would have known anyway, such as the layout of houses, her father's car, the trips and spins and the existence of a 'secret wood'.

'Apart from your sister, you are the only person who can say what happened when Melissa died,' he said.

Samantha agreed that this was the case and said she had no doubt that her sister had been present and had also witnessed what she had witnessed.

'She gave a different version of what happened. She had spoken to Dad on the phone and was so brainwashed by him. He has control over her and she changed her statement a number of times,' Samantha said of her sister.

Mr Grehan wanted to know if Jill had been in touch with their father since his arrest in April 2008. Samantha said he had telephoned her from prison and she had sent him a card for his birthday.

'Have you spoken to your sister about what happened?' asked Mr Grehan.

'No, it's something you wouldn't bring up in conversation.'

'Was it discussed that night?'

'No, he gave us money.'

'Did you talk about it by typing text messages and passing a mobile phone to each other?'

'No, not that I remember.'

'You've told us everything?'

'Yes.'

'And you didn't tell anyone until January 31, 2008?'

'That's correct.'

Mr Grehan then asked Samantha when she had stopped living with her father and she replied that he had kicked her out of the house a number of times. She said he had beaten her up on one occasion and thrown her out. In September 2007, she had been living on the streets and getting into trouble with gardaí. She said that her father had been worried about the police getting to him through her.

'I used to rob out of Tesco to get my dad in trouble. He'd have to come to the garda station to get me out. He said I was taking drugs, but I wasn't. He was taking them.'

She was asked if she had taken drugs in the past, including cocaine, and agreed that she had done when she used to go out drinking with her friends.

Mr Grehan asked her about her relationship with Jill, and Samantha said they got along 'ok'. 'We had fights. All sisters have fights. She was more for Dad. She was in love with him, obsessed by him, would have stuck up for him.'

'Were the fights serious?'

'No.'

Samantha agreed that her sister had been initially friendly with Melissa and Leeanna Mahon and that she had not liked them at first. She said that the only reason for her dislike had been that the Mahons had been getting Jill into trouble.

'Did you think they were cocky and stuck up?'

'No, they weren't stuck-up girls.'

'So, you didn't think they were smart and cocky?'

'No.'

Mr Grehan then read from Samantha's pre-trial statement to gardaí in which she said: 'I didn't like them because they were smart and cocky.' She explained to the court that she had said that because the girls behaved that way towards her sister, Shirley, but not to her.

Mr Grehan said that Samantha had started hanging around with Melissa and getting into trouble for 'dossing'. They had been suspended from school and, even though Melissa was younger than Samantha, they had continued to spend time together. Jill had struck up the friendship and had invited the Mahons to the Dunbar house but she then had become sidelined as Samantha and Melissa's friendship grew.

'She used to call me her sister,' said Samantha.

'Did she call your dad, her dad?'

'Yes, but that was only a cover-up.'

Samantha told the jury that Melissa had said that she had been sexually abused by her own father. Melissa had made the allegation 'a good bit into the friendship, before she ran away from home'.

Samantha said that, on the morning Melissa had first run away from her own home, she had been asleep in bed when she had heard someone banging on the front door. Mary and Leeanna Mahon were at the door looking for Melissa. Samantha had found Melissa in the house and they had gone to hide in the shed in the garden. She said Melissa had been afraid of her mother and when Mary Mahon had found the girls' hiding place, she had smacked Melissa in the face and Melissa had 'peed' herself.

Samantha agreed that, at some stage in 2006, her father had barred Melissa from the house because she had been cheeky to him, but she had soon started coming back. Samantha knew that the second time Melissa had run away from home, in August 2006, she had stayed at the Dunbar house for three weeks. She was aware that her father had told Garda Pat Conway that he could search the house during that time and she remembered gardaí had actually carried out a search of her home on 14 or 15 September 2006.

In relation to 31 January 2008, Samantha insisted that it was she who had mentioned Melissa Mahon to her sister, Shirley, first. Mr Grehan suggested that Shirley had asked her directly if she knew something about what had happened to Melissa Mahon and had asked if their father had killed her. In Samantha's version, she had said, 'I have to tell you something about Dad and Melissa', and Shirley had replied that she thought she knew what her sister was 'going on about'.

Samantha told Mr Grehan that her younger sister had been brainwashed by their father. She said she was aware of some of the things Jill had said had happened. She said that Jill's first statement had been a result of their father ringing the girl and telling her to blame Samantha. She said that Jill had told her that he had done that. Jill took all the blame herself in another statement.

'She ultimately gives a very similar account to the one you gave,' said Mr Grehan.

Samantha said that the account that Jill had given that was similar to her own was not given as the result of being brainwashed. Samantha had made her first statement to gardaí on 1 February 2008 and, on the same day, had shown detectives the route to the spot where Melissa's body had been dumped. She had made a cautioned statement on 2 February and further statements on 5 March and 3 May 2008. Gardaí had given

Samantha her statements to review before she gave evidence but she said she had not read over them.

'It's very stressful to read over that. Do you not think I have been through enough?' she asked Mr Grehan.

It is common for a witness to refresh their memory outside the court and before going into the witness box by reading any statements they had previously made to gardaí. Professionals, such as doctors and gardaí, are allowed to refer to their notes while in the witness box if the court's permission has been sought first and the court is satisfied that the notes were made at the time of the incident about which the professional is giving evidence. The use of notes is only allowed to assist witnesses who would be involved in a large number of cases where it would be unreasonable to expect them to remember the details of each case. Civilian witnesses may not bring memory aids into the box and the defence should be informed that the witness has had access to their previously made statement.

A previously made statement is not generally admissible in a trial as evidence of what is stated within it, except in exceptional circumstances when certain requirements are met or agreements are made between the prosecution and defence. A pre-trial statement can be used by the cross-examining party to explore any differences between what a witness had told gardaí earlier and what they tell the jury during the trial. Material changes in what a witness had said happened can be highlighted in an attempt to damage a witness' credibility.

Samantha told Mr Grehan that before Melissa had run away from her own home, she had told the Dunbars about what had been going on with her parents and had said that she did not want to live with them.

'She wanted to be part of your family then?' asked Mr Grehan.

'She was actually Dad's girlfriend,' Samantha replied. 'I was actually in the house when they used to be doing it.'

'Did you ever see them?'

'Yes, Melissa and Dad were upstairs and I saw them in Dad's bedroom having sex.'

'That's not in your statements. Did you say anything?'

'What can you say? I was disgusted,' she replied.

Samantha said that Melissa had told her about the relationship with her father before she had witnessed anything between them. As an explanation for why she had not previously mentioned seeing them having sex, she told the court, 'I put my hands up. I made a mistake. I was upset and confused. I was only a child and it was upsetting going over the same thing again and again.'

Mr Grehan asked Samantha about the conversation she had told the jury she had had with Melissa about Melissa having a relationship with Dunbar. A conversation that Samantha had said her father had overheard.

'He told me to keep quiet about it. Sure what else can he say? He was caught out.'

Mr Grehan said that such a conversation 'simply never happened' and commented that it 'beggars belief' that it could have happened. Samantha replied that Dunbar was the sort of man who would actually have had such a conversation with his daughter.

'You don't know my father. I do. I lived with him for fifteen years of my life.'

Counsel asked Samantha how she got along with Health Service Executive staff at Lis na nÓg when Melissa had been a resident there and she said that she had got along 'ok' with them but had been sent home one day because she had been there too often.

Mr Grehan wanted to know if Samantha had fallen out with Melissa after the incident at Hazel Wood when Melissa had run off into the woods, sniffing gas out of a lighter and Dunbar had had to call gardaí. Samantha said they had not fallen out as far as she could remember.

Mr Grehan referred to Samantha's statement in which she said that Melissa was, at that stage, hanging around with the wrong crowd. Samantha had told gardaí in her pre-trial statement that they did not see as much of Melissa after the Hazel Wood incident because they were 'pissed off' with her. Samantha admitted to the court that she had been annoyed with Melissa that day.

'He is my dad. I do love my dad. I was pissed off that she was treating my dad like a piece of crap, basically.'

Samantha said that Melissa had been hanging around with a boy and girl who were also residents at Lis na nÓg, and another local girl who was going out with the boy. They had all stayed in the Dunbar house on a night Dunbar had been in hospital. A teenage girl who lived on the Rathbraughan Estate, and who was friendly with Ronnie, had told him about it. Samantha said that girl had been his 'spy'. Dunbar had been very unhappy about the teenagers being in his house when he was not there and Samantha told the court that, during an altercation with the boy outside the care home, the boy had threatened Dunbar.

'He threatened to shoot my dad with a replica gun. He said he would get it off his brother.'

Mr Grehan then asked Samantha if she had ever played with an Ouija board and she said that she had, with Melissa, Leeanna and Jill. Dunbar had found out and had told them they had let demons into the house but that he would be able to fight them. Samantha said that while the girls had been playing with the board, the glass had started to move—she had thought it was one of the girls doing it—and had spelled out 'hang Ron'. Samantha said she had screamed and that they had all been frightened.

Samantha told the court that, on the evening that she had seen Melissa being taken to a foster home, the social worker, Donna McTague, had told her that Melissa had locked herself in a bathroom and had cut her arms and was being taken to foster care. Samantha had seen gardaí take Melissa out of the house and put her into a patrol car. She said Melissa had opened the car door and had run but the garda had caught up to her and brought her back to the vehicle.

Samantha then said that her father had told her that Melissa had told him that an old man had drugged her when she had left the foster home. Mr Grehan said that, in her statement, Samantha had said that the old man only said that Melissa had called Dunbar her father and asked the accused to come and collect her from his house. Dunbar had shown Samantha a text message from Melissa that said: 'I'm with Catherine. I'm safe.'

The next time Samantha had seen Melissa was the day after the

Dunbars had moved from number 64 to number 63 Rathbraughan Park. She said that she had been shown the text message on the day they moved. On the following day, she had spotted Melissa in the box bedroom of number 64. Mr Grehan told Samantha that his client had said that that had never happened and that he had not given Melissa a key to the back door of the old house.

'How did she get in then?' asked Samantha.

Samantha denied that she had made a copy of the keys to number 64. She said that when Dunbar had been in hospital, the back door key had been lost and she had gone to the letting agent to request a replacement but they had refused to give her one. Mr Grehan suggested to her that if Melissa had been in number 64, then she was there because Samantha had had a key and had let her in. Samantha refused to accept that hypothesis.

Mr Grehan asked Samantha where Melissa had slept the night she had borrowed the Beauty and the Beast nightdress but Samantha said she did not know.

'Hold on,' said Mr Grehan, 'she was your friend.'

'She was also my dad's girlfriend,' replied Samantha.

Mr Grehan said he could not believe Samantha was serious when she said she did not know where Melissa had slept that night. Samantha said she had gone to bed first.

During this part of the cross-examination, Samantha's story began to come unstuck. She had been calm and certain in her evidence up until the issue of who slept where on that particular night in September was explored.

Samantha initially told Mr Grehan that she had gone to bed at around 8 p.m. or 9 p.m. and had slept in the big bedroom at the back of the house. She thought that Jill was at Angelique Sheridan's flat that night but that Jill had come home to Rathbraughan Park after she had gone to bed.

But, if Samantha had slept in the big bedroom that night, how did she manage to see Melissa standing at the window of that same room, watching Dunbar in the garden, the following morning?

Samantha replied that she had moved into another bedroom in the middle of the night. It was an odd explanation and an exchange occurred between the witness and the barrister for some minutes in which Mr Grehan became increasingly incredulous as Samantha tried to explain a musical beds scenario that just did not add up. The confusion over where Samantha had slept that night seemed to surprise even Mr Grehan who had perhaps not thought that it would be this issue that would trip up the witness so badly. Samantha excused herself by saying, 'I'm getting confused because I am getting questions fired at me.'

On the subject of beds, Mr Grehan suggested to Samantha that it was, in fact, she who had cut the hole in the base of the divan bed in order to have somewhere to hide items she had stolen from shops. She agreed that she had taken make-up and sweets from shops and pharmacies but she said she had been marched back to the shop to return the items by her father when he had found out what she had done.

'You made a hole under the bed to hide the stuff you had taken?'

'I know there was a hole in the bed, that's what my father had done. I didn't make that hole.'

Mr Grehan then turned to the evening of Melissa's death when Samantha had talked about coming home from Youth Reach and walking into the house. Samantha agreed that she had had no key and said her father had left the door on the latch.

'So anyone could walk in?' asked Mr Grehan.

'Yes.'

'Are you sure you didn't have to knock to get into the house?'

'I'm sure. The door was open.'

Samantha said her sister was crying and smoking a 'Superking fag' and had told Samantha not to go upstairs. Samantha said she had not asked Jill why she was crying as 'she always used to cry'. She said her sister had asked her not to go upstairs but Samantha's natural reaction to such a remark meant that 'obviously' she had gone up, exactly because she had been told not to. Her father's bedroom door had been closed, but not locked. She said that he had been aware that she had walked into the room. Although the room had been dark, there had been enough light to see Melissa and Dunbar lying on the bed.

Samantha said that while she could see her father's arm around Melissa's neck, she couldn't see whether or not it was around her neck tightly.

'I didn't think anything of it. I thought he was giving her a hug,' she said.

Mr Grehan told the court that, in Samantha's first statement to gardaí, she had said that she had walked out of the room thinking that Melissa was asleep and that her father was hugging her.

'You don't describe a violent holding on to her neck,' said Mr Grehan.

'I wasn't there when it started,' said Samantha.

'What you saw was your father's arm positioned in a friendly fashion. You didn't see him inflict any violence on Melissa.'

'No.'

'Did he do anything else violent to her?'

'No.'

'There's no question of him smothering her with a pillow?' asked Mr Grehan.

'I didn't see him smothering her,' replied Samantha.

'You didn't see him wrap a tie around her neck and get you to pull one end and your sister the other?'

'No.'

'You don't know what might have gone on before you got there?'

'No.'

Mr Grehan told Samantha that what she had described was like a silent movie. According to Samantha's account, no one had spoken, no one had asked any questions.

'Everyone was in shock. You don't really chat when you're in shock. No one screamed. He wasn't shouting,' Samantha said.

Mr Grehan wanted to know what had caused Samantha's decision to resuscitate Melissa, if it was the case that she had not seen her father do anything violent to her friend and no one had said a word or had explained the situation. Samantha agreed that she had not seen any marks on Melissa's neck.

'So how was it that you came to do something like that?'

Samantha said she had been able to see that Melissa's chest was moving and that she was struggling to breathe. Samantha had learned how to perform resuscitation at Youth Reach. She said she had got on to the bed, kneeled on top of Melissa's legs and pressed below her chest with both hands two or three times. Melissa's chest had been moving up and down but it stopped. The attempted resuscitation was not working so Samantha had moved away.

'I was in shock. I didn't know what to do,' she said.

'Why didn't you ask him what had happened?' asked Mr Grehan.

'I didn't ask questions. I was in shock.'

Mr Grehan confirmed that while Dunbar was downstairs, Samantha had been in the room with Melissa for a couple of minutes and had not seen any sign of injury on her.

'You asked no questions? You just hopped up on the bed and started compressions on her chest?' asked Mr Grehan.

'Yes,' replied Samantha. 'I didn't know if she was dead or not. She was trying to breathe but she stopped after I stopped. I started to cry.'

'Why did you think he was going to put Melissa into a sleeping bag?'

'Why else would he bring it up?'

'You don't know how she died,' said Mr Grehan.

'I wasn't there at the start,' agreed Samantha.

'You knew nothing about what went on,' he said. 'You saw very little, other than Melissa trying to breathe.'

Samantha again said that she had been in shock. He father had said nothing to her or to Jill. He had put Melissa into the sleeping bag and the two girls had stood watching him.

'Dad is a very dominant man. I was scared of him. Jill was scared of him. You have to remember I was only fifteen at the time,' Samantha told the court.

She said that he had taken a neck tie from the wardrobe, had put Melissa head first into the sleeping bag and had tied the bag where Melissa's feet were. Still, no one had said anything. Dunbar had lifted the girl down the stairs easily. Samantha said he was a big, strong man and Melissa had been very small, petite and skinny. He had had no trouble carrying her. He had placed her at the bottom of the stairs whilst he had reversed his car closer to the door. Samantha said she had known where they were going when he had started driving because it was a route they had taken many times. Still, there had been no conversation on the way out to the river.

Mr Grehan wanted to know if, and how, Samantha knew Melissa was dead when her father had put her into the boot. She said he had shoved her into the boot and she thought Melissa's neck had broken because she had heard a snap, although she could not be certain it had been her neck because she was not able to see into the sleeping bag. She had thought Melissa was definitely dead because of the 'really strong smell of urine' she had noticed coming from the sleeping bag.

When they had arrived at the 'secret wood' Samantha had a 'fair idea' about what was going to happen. Her father had previously told the girls that no one could find you in the secret wood. She had realised what her father's plan was when they got to entrance to the woods. After he had got the body out of the boot and collected stones the size of golf balls, Dunbar had dragged Melissa across the ground and had told Samantha to help him throw the body into the river.

Samantha told Mr Grehan that she was sure that her father had gone to football practice later that evening, even when counsel told her that another of the players would give evidence that Dunbar had stopped going to the training in August 2006. She said he had definitely been there. It had been his regular 'thing'.

Mr Grehan asked Samantha why she had kept these events secret until the end of January 2008, even though she had been in the garda station many times in the intervening period and had told the court that she had been getting into trouble deliberately so that her father would have to go to the station. Samantha replied that she had been too scared to say what had happened and that the gardaí had never asked her about Melissa. 'You did not even make an anonymous call to the authorities,' said Mr Grehan. She said she was aware of the appeals for information about her friend but said, 'You don't understand how petrified I was. I was really scared of my father.'

Samantha said that she had had no discussions with her sister, Jill, about what had happened. She said she had known that Jill had told Kirsty, their sister who lived in England, that Samantha had been coked off her head, had hit Melissa with a frying pan and had pushed her into the water. Samantha said her mother, Lisa Conroy, had repeated to her what Jill had told Kirsty. When Samantha had confronted Jill about this, Jill had told her that their father had instructed her to say it.

'Jill was in love with Dad,' said Samantha.

On 31 January 2008, Samantha had finally told her sister, Shirley, what had happened. Mr Grehan said that Danny Lynnott, Shirley's partner, had heard Samantha say that she was going to go to jail over it.

'My dad drummed into our heads that we were accessories and would go to juvenile prison,' she said. 'We were all brainwashed. I got out in time. He told us he could fight demons and that they were in Melissa. Who would tell a child that? You don't know how much he brainwashed us and we actually believed him.'

Mr Grehan suggested to Samantha that, for a couple of years, she had been 'living life a bit on the wild side'. She agreed that this had been the case and that she had been drinking. When asked if she had taken any drugs, she said she had taken cocaine once. She had been caught shop lifting, had been a regular at the garda station, had been suspended from school and had been attending Youth Reach. Still, she reiterated, she had been under her father's control and had been afraid to say anything.

'Up until January 2008, I thought I would go to jail for what happened,' she said.

'Even though you did nothing,' asked Mr Grehan. 'You would have figured out that that was rubbish.'

'You don't understand. I was petrified,' she said. 'I knew what happened was wrong. I wish I had opened up sooner. I was scared.'

Samantha said that after she had moved out of her father's house, she had become free of his control. She accepted that he had thrown her out on several occasions and that she had been taken into the care of the Health Service Executive for a number of months before January 2008.

'Why did you shout, "I'm going to jail"?' insisted Mr Grehan.

'Because he said we were accessories.'

At this point, Mr Justice White interrupted the cross-examination to remark that he was not sure if Samantha was not an accessory after the fact in the eyes of the law.

'As of January 31, 2008,' continued Mr Grehan, 'Did you think you might go to jail?'

'I thought we would all go to jail as accessories,' replied Samantha. 'At the end of the day, he's still my father.'

Mr Grehan then turned to the accounts that Jill had provided to gardaí. She had implicated Samantha in her statement of 13 February 2008. Jill had told gardaí that she had been close to Samantha but that Melissa had told their father how concerned she was about Samantha, because Samantha wanted to stab Jill. Jill had said their father had confronted Samantha about this accusation in front of Melissa and that Samantha had reacted very angrily. Samantha told the court that that had 'never happened'. Jill had also claimed that she had found Samantha in their father's bedroom, taking a phone and €50, which she had told Jill was for Melissa. Again, Samantha told the court that that had never happened.

Jill had also told gardaí that she had seen Samantha the following day on a black bicycle with a bag on the handle bars. Jill had said she had stood in the middle of the road to try to make her sister stop, but that Samantha had swerved around her. When Samantha had returned home that night, she had told Jill that she had been to see Melissa. Jill had said it looked like Samantha had been fighting, her hair had been messy and she had been angry, She had told Jill that she had fought with Melissa and admitted hitting Melissa over the head with a piece of wood.

'No. It never happened,' said Samantha.

Also in her statement, Jill had told gardaí that she had told Samantha that what she had done was sick and had threatened to tell their father. She had said that Samantha had then come into her bedroom in the middle of the night with a kitchen knife in her hand.

'Never happened,' Samantha said. 'I've never threatened Jill. I've never threatened anybody with a knife in my life.'

In Jill's account Samantha had put the knife to her sister's throat. Her first reaction had been to scream but she had not been able because of the knife. Samantha had told her that if she 'ratted', she would stick the knife into her throat. Dunbar had then come into the room and had asked what was going on. Samantha had told him it was nothing, Jill had just had a bad dream. Jill said in her statement that he hadn't seen the knife and that she had been scared but that Samantha had left the room and gone back to bed.

'It never happened,' Samantha said.

Mr Grehan then put Jill's second version of events to Samantha in which Jill had claimed that all three of them had had a hand in strangling Melissa. She had said the crime had happened downstairs in their house on Thursday, 21 September 2006. Jill had said that Samantha had been at Youth Reach and Jill had gone to see Angelique Sheridan in the morning. Later, Jill had gone to McDonald's with her pregnant sister, Shirley, but that Shirley had been in pain so they had gone to the hospital. When Jill had got home in the afternoon, Melissa was there with Dunbar. Jill had said that Melissa had been aggressive and angry. She had been shouting about 'f****** social workers' and taking her anger out on Jill and Dunbar. Jill had claimed Melissa had started to slap her but her father had stepped in and stopped her. Jill had then said she had put her hands around Melissa's neck and had started to squeeze.

'Do you remember Thursday, September 21?' asked Mr Grehan.

'I remember a Thursday, but I don't know the date. It was the Thursday after Melissa had run away from care.'

Jill had said Samantha had arrived home from Youth Reach at around 5 p.m. and had let herself in with her key. Samantha told the court that that was wrong, that she hadn't had a key to the house.

Jill had said their father had had his hands around Melissa's throat for around three minutes before Samantha had come in to find him and Jill standing and Melissa lying on the floor at the living-room door. Jill had told Samantha that Melissa had attacked her and their father, and Samantha had called Melissa a 'bitch', knelt down beside her and had put her hands around Melissa's throat for three or four minutes. Jill had thought Melissa was dead by that point, she was not moving and her eyes were closed. Samantha had grabbed the sleeping bag that Melissa had slept in on the sofa the previous night and the three of them had put her body into it. Dunbar had tied the bottom of the bag and had said they should put the body into the boot of the car. Samantha had opened the boot and Dunbar put the body into it without difficulty.

'That's all made up in her head,' said Samantha.

In Jill's account, when they had got to the bank of the river, Dunbar had told Samantha that if the body did not sink Samantha would have to jump into the water and make it go down. Samantha had agreed that this was actually said. She said he would not have told Jill to go into the water.

'He said I would have to go in. Jill was my dad's favourite.'

Mr Grehan pointed out that in a statement she had made to gardaí in March 2008, she had said that her father had thrown stones at the body in the water and had said that if it didn't go down, one of the girls—Samantha or Jill—would have had to go in.

'I can't remember if Jill was asked or not.'

Gardaí had asked Samantha on 1 February 2008 if she had ever returned to the place where Melissa's body had been dumped. She had told them that her father had asked her if she wanted to go back to the place where they had 'bumped off' Melissa. Jill had told Samantha that she had gone back to the River Bonet with their father. Samantha agreed with Mr Grehan that her sister and father had gone back to the scene but she said that she had not.

'So you did discuss events with Jill,' asked Mr Grehan. 'You said you and Jill never discussed what happened.'

'We never discussed the murder. She told me she went back,' replied Samantha.

Mr Grehan told Samantha that Jill had gone back to gardaí on 2 July 2008 after their father had been charged with murder and was being held at Castlerea Prison. She had told gardaí that she wanted to tell the truth, that their father had killed Melissa. She said she was not going to protect him anymore. Mr Grehan put Jill's third statement to Samantha.

Jill had told gardaí that, on 21 September, she had been making a cake downstairs and had decided to go upstairs either to give a cigarette to Melissa or to get one from her. She had gone into her father's bedroom for no particular reason and had seen him on top of Melissa, they were lying on the double bed fully clothed and facing each other. Melissa had been wearing a Beauty and the Beast nightdress and Jill had asked her father what he was doing. He had said he was keeping Melissa sweet. Jill had not been sure what this meant but had thought that, perhaps, Melissa had threatened to go to the gardaí about the relationship they were having. Jill had heard Melissa laugh and had then gone back downstairs.

According to Jill, five minutes later, Samantha had knocked on the front door and Jill had let her in. Jill had said she was upset and had been wondering what her father was doing. Perhaps they were having sex, but she had never seen them doing that before. She had asked Samantha to come with her and look at what was happening and so Samantha had followed her upstairs.

Samantha told the court that she disagreed with certain parts of the statement. She said that she had let herself into the house, had found Jill in tears and had gone upstairs first. She agreed with what Jill had then said about what they had seen when they had gone into their father's bedroom.

The girls were in agreement about the position of Dunbar and Melissa on the bed and about what they had been wearing. They agreed that their father's arm was around Melissa's neck but Samantha denied that he had ordered them out of the room. She was certain that he had said nothing. Jill, on the other hand, had told gardaí that her father had said that Melissa was going to go to the gardaí and that she had tried to stab him.

Samantha also disagreed with Jill about where the tie had been taken from. Jill had said it had come from the bedside cabinet, whereas Samantha said he had taken it from the wardrobe.

Samantha denied that her father had put the tie around Melissa's neck and told them to hold either end. She was also at odds with Jill when Jill had said that their father had put a pillow over Melissa's face. It simply did not happen that way according to Samantha.

Mr Grehan then put a number of propositions to Samantha which she also denied.

'Your father never had any relationship of an untoward nature of any kind with Melissa Mahon.'

'He did.'

'Melissa was not in your house at all after September 14.'

'She was. He's lying.'

'He never gave her a key to any house.'

'He did.'

'Your father had no involvement in the killing of Melissa Mahon.'

'He's a liar. We couldn't drive ourselves.'

'You didn't, in fact, see your father inflict any violence on Melissa,' said Mr Grehan.

'He had his arm around her neck. I thought he was hugging her. He's trying to wriggle his way out,' she replied. 'I'm trying to tell you he is lying. I don't know what happened before I went into the room.'

'You have not told us the full truth of what you know.'

'I have.'

'The account you've given is totally unbelievable.'

Ms Kennedy interrupted Mr Grehan to point out that his last remark was entirely a matter for the jury.

Mr Grehan continued, 'What you describe is a silent movie.'

Samantha said, 'I wouldn't call it a movie now.'

'You have put yourself in the role of heroine. You tried to resuscitate Melissa, without any inquiry into what was going on.'

'Remember I was only fifteen years of age, a young girl,' Samantha countered.

'You have concocted an unbelievable account because you have not been able to deal with the truth of what happened,' said Mr Grehan.

'I have been able to deal with the truth,' she replied.

12 | JILL'S EVIDENCE

The defence was finally finished with Samantha by lunch-time on the 10th day of the trial. She had been in the box for two and a half days and it then became the turn of her younger sister, Jill, to give evidence. Jill was born in September 1992 and was 13 years old, just about to turn 14, when Melissa was reported missing. At the time she gave evidence to the Central Criminal Court in May 2009, she was 16 years old and, therefore, could not be named and could testify via live television link.

Dunbar had had an idea about what Samantha would say, but Jill was more of an unknown quantity. When Samantha had cracked and told gardaí where Melissa's remains could be found, Jill had initially stood by her father. He must have hoped that her love for him, and his control over her, would damage the prosecution case to the point where the jury would not be convinced that Samantha had told the truth. Jill had given a number of different accounts to gardaí about what had happened, variously blaming herself, her sister and her father for Melissa's death. Her evidence would throw up a number of problems for the prosecution. There would be discrepancies about Melissa's last moments that would be difficult for the jury to reconcile.

Dressed in a blue blazer and red top, Jill appeared on screen that afternoon with the same degree of composure that

Samantha had displayed. She, too, had a strong English accent and spoke firmly and clearly. She told Ms Kennedy that in late June or early July 2008, she had contacted Sligo Garda Station to make a new and final statement about what had happened to Melissa. She had made several earlier statements but they had not been the correct version of events and she had felt it was time to set the record straight. She was going to tell the truth for her own protection and for her friend Melissa. She wanted to tell the court what had really happened—that her father had murdered Melissa Mahon.

Jill told Ms Kennedy that on 20 September 2006, which was a Wednesday, she had accompanied her pregnant sister, Shirley, to hospital. Shirley had thought she was in labour but had been mistaken and Jill had left her at the hospital around lunch-time when her sister's partner, Danny, had arrived. Jill had then gone to look for Angelique Sheridan but could not find her so had gone home to Rathbraughan Park. When she had arrived at her house, she had knocked on the door to be let in. She had had to wait a number of minutes before her father had opened the door. When he had eventually let her in, Jill had followed him out to the back garden. She had seen him leaning over the back wall into the house next door, number 64, where they had originally lived. Dunbar had moved himself and his daughters into number 63 about a week earlier. Jill had wanted to know what was going on, she thought he might have been dumping rubbish, so she had looked over the wall and had seen Melissa Mahon. She was kneeling on the ground with a key in her hand stretching towards the back door of number 64.

Jill had got angry with her father when she saw Melissa. He had been told not to have her in his house and he was going to get into trouble. Jill told the court that, in August, Melissa had stayed with her family in number 64 for three weeks after she had run away from her own home and before going into care at Lis na nÓg. Melissa had originally been her friend at the Mercy College but had become closer to Samantha and had got along extremely well with their father. Jill had often seen Melissa and her father lying on the sofa under a blanket together in the old house. Jill had heard that Melissa had run away from the foster home she had been taken to. She told Ms Kennedy that she did not remember hearing about a phone call to her father in the early hours of that morning when Melissa had bolted from the foster family's house.

After looking over the wall, Jill had been upset and had retreated into number 63 and run upstairs. She had sat crying on the stairs and had told her father, when he came into the house, that he was going to get into trouble. He had told her to shut up.

That evening, Jill had been in number 63 with her father, Samantha and Melissa when Shirley had called to the house. Melissa had hidden behind the living-room door but Shirley had spotted her and left the house. Later, a garda had arrived at the front door and Melissa had run out into the back garden, climbed over the back wall and gone into number 64. Dunbar had let the garda in to look for Melissa but he hadn't been able to find her there, so he had left.

When it was time for bed on the night before Jill said Melissa died, Jill had gone to the box room upstairs and Samantha had gone to her room at the back of the house. Jill said that Melissa had stayed downstairs on the sofa in the living room. The next morning, Thursday, 21 September, Jill had woken up at 8 a.m. Melissa, Samantha and her father had been in the house and Samantha had been getting ready to go to Youth Reach. Dunbar had been up but Jill had seen Melissa in his bedroom, lying in the double bed. She had been wearing a yellow nightdress with a Beauty and the Beast motif, a pair of black trousers and a pair of socks. Jill had been in the second year at Mercy College but had not gone to school that day. When Jill had asked her father what Melissa was doing in his bed, he had said that she had woken up in the middle of the night, gone up to his bed and was now sleeping.

Father and daughter had gone out to buy groceries in Lidl and when they got back to Rathbraughan Park, Melissa was still there, wearing the same clothes. Samantha had already gone to Youth Reach. A friend of Dunbar's had called to the house that afternoon and Melissa had run upstairs out of sight because she had known she could not be seen there. Jill had seen Melissa hiding under a blanket in the box room. When the friend had left, Dunbar had gone upstairs to Melissa, and Jill had gone to the kitchen to bake a cake.

Later, Jill had decided to see what was going on so had gone upstairs. Her father's bedroom door had been open so she had gone into the room. There, she had seen her father lying on top of Melissa on the bed. Melissa had been lying diagonally across the bed on her back and Dunbar had been on top of, and facing, her. They were both fully dressed. Jill had asked him what he was doing and he had looked up and said he was 'keeping her sweet'. Jill told the court that Melissa had laughed.

She said she had left the room and gone back downstairs. It was around 5 p.m. and Samantha was due home from Youth Reach. Ten minutes after Jill had seen her father lying on top of Melissa, Samantha had knocked on the front door and Jill had let her in to the house. Jill told the court she had been upset, but she wasn't crying. She had told Samantha to go upstairs and look at what was going on.

The sisters had gone into their father's bedroom. Jill said she had seen her father lying side by side with Melissa, with both their heads at the top of the bed near the headboard. They had been on top of the bed clothes and Melissa had had her back to Dunbar and had been on her side. He had been behind her, also on his side, facing her back. His right forearm had been around her neck and he had been strangling her. Jill had remembered which arm it was because he wore bracelets on his right arm. Melissa's arms were down by her sides. Jill said she had been some distance into the room and Samantha had been at the door. She said her father had told them to get out. Melissa was not moving or speaking and her eyes were closed. The bedroom light was off and the curtains were closed but they were made from a light fabric and there was enough light coming through them to enable Jill to see.

Jill told the court that her father had then said that Melissa had tried to kill him and had threatened to go to the gardaí.

He had stayed on the bed for a little while longer and then had got up. Jill said the light in the bedroom had now been turned on and her father had got a blue tie from his side cabinet. Shirley had bought him the tie and he had worn it the previous Christmas. She said that he had put it around Melissa's neck and asked Jill and Samantha to each hold an end of the tie while he went to the bathroom. Melissa was, by now, lying on her back, her eyes were still closed.

Jill said she had gone downstairs to get the dogs and her father had remained upstairs. Before she had left the room, she had seen Melissa's body moving up and down and had heard her making a faint moaning sound. She told the court that she had been scared and confused. Her mind had been pretty blank except for the thought that she had to turn off the oven. She told Ms Kennedy that she had thought her father and Melissa were faking what she was witnessing. She had thought it was not real, that he was not really killing Melissa. The 13 year old had thought that her 14 year old friend was going to wake up and start laughing.

Jill said she had gone back upstairs. Her father had been in the toilet but then had gone back into the bedroom. There was no conversation. The tie had still been around Melissa's neck and Jill said he had then taken a pillow and had placed it over Melissa's face as his two daughters stood and watched. He had turned to Samantha and had told her to go and get a sleeping bag. Her sister did as she was told and got the sleeping bag that Melissa had been using on the sofa the night before.

Dunbar had put Melissa's body into the sleeping bag head first and then asked Jill and Samantha to help him. Jill said she had then been ordered downstairs to check if anyone was outside. Her father had come down the stairs, carrying Melissa's body in the sleeping bag, and had gone out to his car which had been in front of the house. Jill thought he might have made Samantha help him carry the body, but she wasn't sure. He had put Melissa's body into the boot, closed it and had told the girls to get into the car. Jill said she had got into the back of the car and Samantha had sat in the front passenger seat.

He had driven for 20 minutes to a spot along the River Bonet. They had been there during the summer and had planned to camp there at some stage. When her father had stopped the car, he told Jill to get out and see if anyone was around. When he had been sure the coast was clear, he had got out of the car and opened the boot. Jill said he had then got Samantha to help him lift Melissa's body out of the car. He had dragged the sleeping bag along the ground to the edge of the water and unzipped it. Jill said he had taken the tie from around Melissa's neck, zipped up the bag again and had tied the neck tie around the top of the bag. While the bag had been open, Jill had seen Melissa's body. She said it had looked normal on one side but had appeared to be purple and blue on the other. Her father had then told Samantha to help him swing the sleeping bag into the water. No one had said anything. They had got back into the car and had driven back to Sligo. Dunbar had warned his daughters that they were accessories to murder—and they had believed him.

Jill told the court that she thought it was 6 p.m. when they had returned to Rathbraughan Park. Her father had been due to go to his usual Thursday night football practice in Collooney a friend of her father's had arrived at the house in a red sports car to take him to training. Samantha and Jill had gone with him as usual that evening and had watched him play. Jill said that, that evening, she had said to her father, 'Don't kill me if I'm bad.'

At this point in Jill's evidence, Ms Kennedy asked a garda to take the sleeping bag and nightdress which had been found at Lough Gill into the room in the Four Courts from where Jill was giving her live evidence. When shown the items, Jill was able to identify them as the sleeping bag her father had used to dump Melissa's body and the nightdress she had last seen Melissa wearing.

Jill said that one morning in March 2007, she had been woken by her father in the early hours. He had wanted to visit the place where he had dumped Melissa's body to see if it had surfaced. Jill said she hadn't known why her father had brought her with him on this grim trip. They had returned to the spot along the River Bonet in Dunbar's car. He had taken an inflatable rubber dinghy out of the back of the vehicle and had pumped it up with a hand pump. They had walked down the path and placed the dinghy into the water. Jill had been told to get into the boat and he had climbed in behind her with a set of oars. He had brought a torch and used it to examine the river. They were there for an hour, rowing up and down the River Bonet until 3 a.m.

After this, it was Jill's turn to be cross-examined and Mr Grehan opened by saying that she knew her father had denied that he was involved in the killing of Melissa Mahon. Mr Grehan said Jill had made several different statements to gardaí. She had suggested that Samantha was involved in Melissa's death and that she, herself, was also responsible before she had given the account that the court had just heard. He said she had spoken to gardaí just two weeks before the trial had started in April 2009. He asked her if she was aware that her account differed from Samantha's. He said that if they had both been present when Melissa had died, and had witnessed what had happened, one might well expect small discrepancies but the major events should be the same. Jill's reply was that that people perceive things differently.

She said she had a clear memory of the night when her father had put Melissa into a sleeping bag and had dumped her body. She denied that she had jumbled up the sequence of events to any great extent. Perhaps a few things were in the wrong order, maybe the conversations.

Mr Grehan asked Jill if she had telephoned her aunt, Judy Dunbar, the accused's sister, the previous week to tell her that Samantha had been lying in the witness box. She said that she did not remember doing that. Jill said she had mentioned the court case to her aunt but hadn't talked about her sister. When asked if she was aware of her sister's evidence in court, she said that she only knew what Samantha had said by reading what had appeared in the newspapers during the trial. Jill remarked that the papers add things in and take things out. Mr Grehan said she was 'quite right'.

Jill was asked if she was absolutely sure that her father had tied a neck tie around Melissa's neck. She said she was. Jill said she had not been aware that Samantha had denied that that particular incident had happened and had said that she would have remembered it if it had. Jill said that she was not, however, surprised that Samantha had said that it hadn't happened. Jill said she and her sister saw things differently. Maybe Samantha did not remember that it had happened, but it definitely had. Mr Grehan argued that both girls could not be right about whether or not the tie had been used around Melissa's neck. They could not both be mistaken about something so graphic.

It was the end of the court day, but Mr Grehan was far from finished with the witness. Jill returned to the Four Courts the following morning for further cross-examination. Mr Grehan again raised the issue of the neck tie. Jill continued to insist that her father had ordered his daughters to hold each end of the tie and pull. She said that she had not really known what she was doing and had been too frightened to ask. She couldn't remember if the tie had been tight around Melissa's neck and she did not know if Melissa had been breathing or moving at that stage. Jill said she thought Melissa had been unconscious but that her chest had been moving up and down. The tie had seemed to stop her breathing. Her father had left the room but the girls had continued to hold the tie. Jill was asked why they hadn't let go. She said that she had been frightened. She had told Ms Kennedy that she had left the room after a number of minutes to go downstairs to turn the oven off.

'Are you serious about that?' asked Mr Grehan.

'I'm very serious,' she replied.

'How do you explain that Samantha said that none of this had happened?'

'That was Samantha's statement.'

Mr Grehan again told her that they could not both be right. Jill replied that both statements had said that their dad had killed Melissa and had disposed of her body. She said people perceive things differently, especially when they are in shock.

When asked how she could she have thought it had been a joke or a game and yet have been terrified by what was happening, Jill said that her father was a very violent and a very volatile man. She agreed that she had never heard of a joke like that one. Mr Grehan asked her if she had heard of other young people doing something like that, stopping their friends from breathing. She said she had not.

Mr Grehan moved on from the discussion of the neck tie and

told Jill that her account had also differed from Samantha's in a number of other respects. Jill said she had not seen her sister since the trial had started. She was asked why she had contacted her Aunt Judy and said that she had discussed something that she could not talk about in court. Jill said she had asked her aunt if she had been in court and if she had chased Shirley's partner, Danny Lynnott, down the stairs calling him a liar. Mr Grehan told Jill that her aunt had not been to the trial at all. Jill again denied that she had told her aunt that Samantha was lying. She said she had telephoned her aunt repeatedly and had been told not to ring again. Jill agreed with Mr Grehan that she had been told not to ring Judy Dunbar again 'if it was the last breath she took'.

Mr Grehan asked Jill if she was sure she had been in 64 Rathbraughan Park the day before she said Melissa had died, because it had been Samantha's evidence that Jill had not come home that night until after Samantha had gone to bed. Jill said that had not been the case because she had not been allowed out late at night. It was another difference in their testimonies.

Mr Grehan pointed out that Samantha had said that Melissa had been standing at a window looking into the garden the following morning, whereas Jill said she had been in her father's bed. Jill had said Samantha had got up before her and argued that Melissa could have gone back to bed.

Counsel then turned to what Jill had said about finding her father on top of the bed with Melissa when he had said, by her account, that he was 'keeping her sweet'. Jill agreed that Melissa had not seemed to be in any trouble or difficulty at that point.

Jill said that Samantha had knocked on the front door to be let in, whereas Samantha's evidence was that she had pushed the door open herself and had found Jill crying in the sitting room, smoking a cigarette. Another difference between the sisters. Jill's explanation, once again, was that people perceive things differently.

Samantha had told the court that Jill had told her not to go upstairs, whereas Jill was sure that she had asked her sister to go upstairs and have a look at what was happening. When asked who went upstairs first, Jill said that it was such a minor detail that she could not remember. She said she wanted to show Samantha that their father was on top of Melissa because it had upset her. Jill said she had gone into the bedroom first, whereas Samantha had said she had entered first and had then walked back out bumping into Jill who had been behind her. Jill said that was wrong and that, to her knowledge, her own account was the correct one.

Jill accepted that before she had gone into the bedroom for a second time, she had not been aware that there was anything wrong with Melissa and when she had walked into the room, it appeared that her father was hugging Melissa in a friendly rather than violent manner. Mr Grehan told Jill that Samantha's evidence was that their father had immediately pulled his arm away from Melissa. He asked Jill if she was saying that she could see his arm being held in a violent fashion. She replied that, after a couple of seconds of looking at his arm, she had been able to sense that it wasn't a cuddle. Whereas Samantha was clear that she had seen nothing violent, Jill was sure that it had been an aggressive position and she had been able to see that her father had been restricting Melissa's neck by the way he held his arm.

'Did you think at that stage that your father had choked Melissa?'

'I didn't know what to think.'

Jill was becoming agitated with the constant highlighting of differences between her account and Samantha's. She told Mr Grehan that he would be more worried if they were telling exactly the same story.

Mr Grehan told Jill that her sister had told the court that no words had been exchanged and that her father had said nothing to them. Jill said that perhaps her sister did not remember.

'Maybe you are making up what you say happened. Maybe what both of you say is untrue,' suggested Mr Grehan.

Jill disagreed. She said she had known that her sister would call her a liar. Mr Grehan said that Samantha had not called her anything of the sort but he still could not understand why there were such differences in their stories about the 'big things'.

He asked Jill if Samantha had attempted to resuscitate Melissa. 'Does that ring any bells?'

Jill could not remember that happening, perhaps she had been downstairs when it had. She disagreed with Samantha's account that she had been crying in the bedroom throughout. Told that Samantha had not seen her father use any pillow, Jill again replied that that had been Samantha's statement, not hers. Maybe Samantha had gone downstairs to get the sleeping bag when her father had been smothering Melissa. 'But,' said Mr Grehan, 'Samantha said it was your father who fetched the sleeping bag.'

'We have different perceptions. It was a long time ago. We were both very young.'

Jill had said Samantha had helped her father to carry Melissa downstairs, but Samantha had said that did not happen. Jill had said that she had sat in the back seat of the car and Samantha had been in the front. Samantha had said the opposite.

Mr Grehan asked Jill if she had seen any injuries on Melissa. She said she had noticed slashes on her arms and said that Melissa was a self-harmer. She was asked if she had seen injuries to Melissa's neck.

'To be honest with you I didn't want to look,' she said.

Mr Grehan then began to explore what had happened in February 2008 when gardaí had become aware of Samantha's version of events. When Jill had been questioned on 1 February, she had said that she knew nothing. She had maintained that attitude the following day. On 13 February, when gardaí had begun to find remains at Lough Gill, Jill had again been asked what she knew and had said that she thought Melissa had received a blow to the head. In court, Jill said that she was not exactly sure what she had initially told gardaí and she had not read over her early false statements.

In those statements, she had said that, in the summer of 2006, her father had told her that Melissa had told him that Samantha wanted to stab and kill Jill. Jill told Mr Grehan that there was another teenage girl who knew what Melissa had said who would give evidence later. Jill said, however, that it had never happened and Samantha had never threatened her with a knife.

In relation to the false statements she had made in early 2008 when she was 15 years old, Jill said she had been frightened and had lied. Her father had been feeding her stories to tell gardaí. She had been terrified for herself and for him and had not wanted him to get into trouble.

'My dad used to put things into my head around the time I was making statements. I tried to protect my dad, which I shouldn't have done. He said he would kill himself, hang himself, which made me very upset. I was frightened for him.'

In one of Jill's early accounts, she had told gardaí that they had been on a camping trip when Melissa had died. In court, she said that was made up but that her father had spoken to her about the trip as though it had really happened. In another early story, Jill had said that she had strangled Melissa along with her father and Samantha by accident. She had told gardaí that it wasn't fair that only one person was getting the blame.

Mr Grehan asked Jill if she had telephoned a radio station but she said she had not.

'Did you have a conversation with someone from a radio station?' he asked.

'No,' Jill replied.

'We have a recording of a conversation you had with a radio reporter from Ocean FM,' said Mr Grehan.

'He rang me,' was her answer.

Jill accepted that she had spoken to radio journalist Niall Delaney from Ocean FM in Sligo in the weeks after Samantha had reported her father to gardaí. She said she had spoken to Mr Delaney briefly but could not remember what she had told him. She agreed that, at that time, she had been aware of what had been published in national newspapers and had known the details of the story that Samantha was telling. During the interview, which was never broadcast, Jill had told the reporter that Melissa's death had had nothing to do with her father and that Samantha had attacked Melissa in a row over drugs during a camping trip. She said Melissa and Samantha had been taking gas or cocaine and Samantha had accused Melissa of stealing money. Jill had claimed to have witnessed Samantha hitting and strangling Melissa as she had lain on the ground. She had said she had whacked Samantha with a piece of wood to get her off Melissa but Samantha had been immune to it. Jill had run away and had hidden under a boat. She had also repeated this story to her sister, Kirsty, and to a solicitor.

Jill told the court that she was disgusted with herself for trying to protect her father because it had all been false. She said her father had told her what to say and, while he did not directly tell her to blame Samantha, he had asked Jill if she had remembered that Samantha had done 'this or that'.

'If someone repeats something to you over and over again, you start to believe it,' she said.

Instead of blatantly telling Jill to cover up what he had done, Dunbar had suggested scenarios to his then 15-year-old daughter, hoping she would implicate her sister. He had been fond of accusing Samantha of taking drugs and had planted the notion in Jill's head that drug use had been behind the killing. Jill told the court that Dunbar had started to believe his own stories. He had repeatedly told himself that he had had nothing to do with Melissa's death and had begun to believe that he was actually innocent. Jill said she had never discussed with her father what had really happened to Melissa. Jill said that the only conversation she had had with him about the true version of events had been when he had told Jill about what Shirley had told the media.

In early February 2008, Jill had been communicating with her father by mobile phone calls and text messages. She told Mr Grehan that he had exerted further emotional control over her when he had texted her saying that he was going to kill himself using a syringe and caustic soda.

It was only when her father had been charged with murder and had been taken into custody that she had felt able to open up and tell the truth.

Jill agreed with Mr Grehan that she had telephoned Childline and had complained that gardaí had been forcing her to make statements. She said she had rung the helpline after she had made her first statement because she had felt uneasy about what was happening and had felt intimidated by the detectives.

She told the court that Judy Dunbar had rung her, shouting, and had told her to tell the gardaí that she and Samantha had killed Melissa. Judy had said she would go to the garda station with Jill to make a new statement and had then told her niece that Ronnie had been crying so much that his eyes were red. Jill said her aunt had been trying to make her feel guilty. Jill accepted Mr Grehan's suggestion that she had told her aunt that she would take the blame because Samantha never would. She also told her aunt that she had been present when Melissa had died and could bring gardaí to the spot where it had happened. Jill said she had been afraid for her father when she said that.

'I don't know why I said it. I'm disgusted with myself.'

She also accepted that she had sent a text messages to friends saying that Samantha had hit Melissa with a lump of wood. Jill had sent a series of text messages to a female friend on 3 February 2008, copies of which the defence had in its possession. In the messages, Jill had said that she was fuming with Samantha and that Samantha had confronted Melissa and hit her with a lump of wood. Jill had written that she had been asleep in the box room of the house in Rathbraughan Park when Samantha had come into the room in the middle of the night and had woken her up. According to the text message, Samantha had had a kitchen knife in her hand and had put it to Jill's throat. She had threatened Jill that if she spoke about what had really happened to Melissa, she would stick the knife into her throat and make it look like Jill had done it to herself. Jill told the friend that Samantha was 'a lunatic'.

In the texts, Jill had also claimed that she had found Samantha stealing €50 from their father's room to give to Melissa and, later the same day, had seen Samantha on a bicycle with two big bags.

Mr Grehan said that in the text messages Jill had clearly been blaming her sister for Melissa's death.

'I was clearly brainwashed,' she replied.

She agreed that she had sent the messages but said that there was no truth in them as she had been brainwashed by her father. She also accepted that she had texted friends saying that she was afraid that Samantha was going to kill her. On 6 February 2008, Jill had sent a text that said that she was not going to take the blame for what had happened and that Samantha could not pass the blame on to her when things got 'too hot'.

The defence had a copy of a text message which had been sent from Jill to Shirley and then forwarded to Detective Garda Pauline McDonagh on 11 April 2008, after Dunbar had been arrested and charged. It stated that Jill had been confused and had truly thought and remembered that Melissa had died downstairs in their house, even though Samantha was saying that it happened upstairs. Asked if what she had said in that text message was true, Jill replied that it was not.

'It was all lies.'

Two days later, on 13 April, Jill had texted her Aunt Judy and said, 'I'll be taking the blame for it all. Dad's not going down, I am. He needs to live the rest of his life.'

Jill told Mr Grehan that he was reading out text messages that had been written and sent by her when she was 'confused and brainwashed'.

'I've told the whole court that I am disgusted with myself. Why go over the past?' she asked the senior counsel.

Jill said it was the statement that she had made to gardaí in July 2008 that had been an accurate account of what had actually happened. She said she was not, at that time, particularly aware of what Samantha had told gardaí, although Mr Grehan pointed out that Shirley had gone to the national press within days of Samantha's confession so she must have known what Samantha had said. Jill said she had seen the article in the *Sunday World* and that newspapers 'twist and turn' the truth so she had paid no heed to what had been written.

'If I knew what Samantha had said then, how come our statements are different?'

Mr Grehan suggested to Jill that the only part of her statement that was consistent with Samantha's was the part which said that their father had had his arm around Melissa's neck. Jill had said other things had been done by her father, such as the smothering with a pillow and the use of a neck tie.

'Your father had nothing to do with the death of Melissa Mahon,' said Mr Grehan.

'So he says,' countered Jill.

'You have not told the truth.'

'I did in July.'

Mr Grehan had finished his cross-examination and had put the defence case to Jill as required—that his client had nothing to do with Melissa's death and that she was a liar.

Ms Kennedy then re-examined Jill to deal with issues that had arisen in Mr Grehan's cross-examination and that the prosecution felt needed to be clarified. She asked Jill again about the use of the neck tie and where it had appeared from. Jill said her father had taken it out a drawer and had put it around Melissa's neck. Ms Kennedy confirmed that it was not Jill's evidence that she had ever seen her father in bed with Melissa before the day Melissa had died. Ms Kennedy said, 'You describe his forearm around her neck.'

'Yes, when I entered the bedroom.'

'You say you saw him strangle her before he left the room.'

'He was lent over the bed and his hands were around her neck, squeezing tightly,' said Jill.

This was not something Jill had said previously and it was the first time the jury, or anyone involved in the investigation, had heard that Dunbar had used his hands to strangle Melissa. Ms Kennedy continued on safer ground. She asked Jill if she usually did what her father told her to do and whether she always believed what her father told her. Jill said she did on both counts. He had made her believe that Samantha had murdered Melissa. The court day drew to a close but, again, Jill would be required to return.

The following morning, in the absence of the jury, Mr Grehan applied to Mr Justice White for an opportunity to cross-examine Jill for a second time. The evidence she had given in re-examination by the prosecution had never been heard before. Mr Grehan had discussed the matter with Ms Kennedy and she had agreed that it was new evidence. He could have looked for a discharge of the jury and a retrial on the grounds that his client had been prejudiced by this testimony but Mr Grehan said he was not seeking to do that. On instructions from Dunbar, he wanted an opportunity to question Jill about this evidence. Mr Justice White granted his application.

Mr Grehan reminded Jill about what she had said in her re-examination by Ms Kennedy. She confirmed that she had said that her father had put his hands around Melissa's neck and had squeezed tightly as he leaned over the bed. She said it had happened before her father had left the bedroom and while Samantha had been in the room.

'You never said this before yesterday. It is not in your so-called "statement of truth",' said Mr Grehan.

Jill replied, 'There are things you remember after, if you try hard.'

'Are you just making this up as you go along?' he asked.

'No. I remembered.'

'But you've never said this before.'

'You remember more when you think hard enough. I remember things every day of the week.'

Mr Grehan told Jill that this new evidence changed what she had previously said had happened but she refused to accept that. She argued that her evidence was essentially the same. She had just remembered more detail.

'This is a fairly big change,' said Mr Grehan.

'No, it's the same,' said Jill.

'We just had his arm around her neck. You then suggested that a tie and a pillow were used and now there is yet another thing, that he actually grabbed her and squeezed her neck in a choking hold.'

Mr Grehan asked when precisely this strangulation had happened. Jill said that it had been after her father had put the tie around Melissa's neck, but before he had told Jill to hold the tie.

'How could you have left this out?' asked Mr Grehan.

'I can't explain it. There are more details to this case, this trial. That's why I told Ms Kennedy,' she replied.

Jill was adamant that she had not added fresh evidence. She had just provided more detail to an account that, she said, was fundamentally the same as it had been before she was re-examined by Ms Kennedy.

'Why didn't you say it before?'

'Ms Kennedy asked me. You didn't ask.'

Mr Grehan laughed and Jill rebuked him for it. She was exasperated with his line of questioning and reminded Mr Grehan if he remembered asking her if she had telephoned a radio journalist and she had said no because it had been the reporter who had telephoned her.

'Yes, you were quite pleased with yourself,' said Mr Grehan.

'What kind of a person do you think I am?' asked Jill. 'I've told the truth.'

'Are there other things you haven't told us about because we haven't asked the right question? When did you recall this new information?'

'When Ms Kennedy was talking to me.'

Mr Grehan told Jill that Samantha had not been asked about this aspect of Jill's evidence. The court had been denied an opportunity to know what she would have said about it. Jill again said that the differences between her own account and her sister's were explained by the fact that people perceive matters differently, coupled with their young ages at the time.

Mr Grehan said that Jill had been in the care of the Health Service Executive since October 2007 and yet she had never mentioned to her social workers what she knew about what had happened to Melissa.

'I went through an upsetting time. I won't go into any more detail than that,' she said.

She said she was not questioned about Melissa's disappearance by social workers or by gardaí and she had continued to have contact with her father by telephone and text message while she was in care. She agreed that she had sent her father a birthday card in September 2008 and had had a long conversation with him in November 2008 when he was in Castlerea Prison. She was asked if she had contacted a radio station in Galway to play messages for her father and she agreed that she had, but not as late as April 2008. She agreed that they had used code names like 'Ali G' and 'Sligo Crew' when making radio requests.

Mr Grehan put further text messages to her that were sent from her phone to her father in February 2008. He said on the 14th, she had written: 'It was all guesswork with me. I didn't do it out of spite. They gave me no other option but to lie.' Jill told the court she had sent the message in fear. The next day she had written: 'I thought I'd get in trouble for seeing Samantha brutally murder Mel.'

'I was frightened,' Jill said. 'Did you get the text from him to me? That he was going to inject himself with caustic soda?'

On 17 February, she had sent a text to her father that asked if she should ring a solicitor. She had also written to tell her father that, because of what had been said in the newspapers, he would not get a fair trial and the case would be dismissed.

'Can I just say I was fifteen and brainwashed.'

Jill told Mr Grehan that her father had telephoned her at that time and told her he was going to cut his wrists. He had also rung her to tell her that he had tried to hang himself but the rope had snapped. She agreed that that information was not in her pre-trial statements.

'It's in other statements that I cannot discuss,' she said.

The prosecution told the court that Jill had, in fact, told gardaí about text messages and phone calls from her father in which he had threatened to harm himself but she had done so in statements that were not pertinent to this particular trial.

In a further text message in February 2008, Jill had written: 'I'd rather me than you. You haven't done anything wrong. I'm lost without you.'

13 | WHAT REMAINED

The prosecution was put in a position where nothing was conceded by the defence so it had to prove that the remains found along the edge of Lough Gill were those of Melissa Mahon.

Lieutenant Commander Brian Hevers, a branch officer with the Irish Naval Service, was called by the State as an expert witness in navigation and charting. He explained how water movement and weather would have impacted on Melissa's body. She would have been in the vicinity for two winters by the time gardaí had searched the area.

On 19 and 20 March 2008, he surveyed the River Bonet from a boat with the assistance of a garda diving unit. He said that the current flowed from the River Bonet into Lough Gill. Lieutenant Commander Hevers was shown the spot where Samantha had indicated that Melissa was placed into the water. The point of entry of the body was secluded and isolated. There was no human habitation in the area and they jury heard that that section of the river would only have been of interest to fishermen. The depth of the water at the bank was two metres but increased quickly to four metres and was as deep as eight metres at its deepest pockets. It was up to 35 metres wide and its bed was muddy with a hard crust. The bed became rocky near the entrance to Lough Gill. Where the river met the mouth of the lake, the ground was very soft and not accessible by foot. The flow of the water into the lake was smooth, steady and clear of obstruction and the speed of that flow depended on the time of year. The area was extremely sheltered at all times of the year and only the northerly end of the river was exposed to the elements.

The river opened into the lake in a northwesterly direction and ran along the shoreline of Lough Gill. Any item coming out of the river would, therefore, be collected along that shoreline. As there was no tide or current flowing through the lake, an object would not be washed out into the lake but would remain within the area known as Bear Rock.

The shore sloped into the lake at a gentle gradient creating shallow water for a considerable distance. The bed of the lake consisted of rocks and boulders so, in Lieutenant Commander Hevers' opinion, if an object moved along that abrasive area it would be badly torn, damaged and broken up. The fact that the items that were recovered by gardaí were found above the water line suggested to him that they had been moved out of the water by animals. Tissue on a body would have attracted the attention of foxes and rats. Lieutenant Commander Hevers said that if a body was placed into the river at the spot indicated by Samantha, it could have travelled into the lake and ended up scattered along the shore within three weeks.

Doctor Jennifer Ryan of the Forensic Science Laboratory in Dublin told the court that she had received a sleeping bag and nightdress on 14 February that had been retrieved from the lake. The sleeping bag had been zipped up and tied at the top with a blue neck tie. The tie had been tied quite tightly and the knot was still in place. She said the sleeping bag had been extensively torn and had a hole of 30 centimetres by 35 centimetres. There was no evidence within it that it had contained a body. There had been some vegetation and debris inside, but no evidence of human decomposition.

The nightdress and sleeping bag had both exhibited damage that was attributed to animal activity and weathering. Nothing on those items suggested that they had contained, or been in contact with, a decomposing body, although they could have been in the water and had obviously been exposed to the elements for some considerable time.

The skeletal remains that had been found along the shoreline near Bear Rock were transported from Sligo to the City Morgue at Marino in Dublin on 13 February 2008 by an undertaker who was escorted by member of An Garda Síochána. Karl Lyon was the senior mortuary technician on duty that day. He had taken possession of the delivery and stored the remains in a fridge with the label 'S2108 unidentified skeletal remains'.

On the sixth day of the trial, the jury was shown a booklet of photographs of the bones which had been taken while they were still in the positions in which they had been found at the water's edge. Mary and Frederick Mahon attended each day of the trial but when these photographs were presented to the jury, Mary left the courtroom in tears. From that moment on, members of the family made it their habit to remove themselves from the hearing when evidence relating to Melissa's remains was being dealt with. Dunbar, on the other hand, flicked through the booklet of photographs as though he was flicking through an Argos catalogue. Anyone who had heard the graphic evidence of what, most likely, had happened to Melissa's body was bound to be upset by it to some degree, yet the man who claimed to have been like a father to Melissa appeared to be utterly unmoved by the grisly details.

On the same day that the remains arrived at the morgue in Dublin, Mary and Frederick Mahon had gone to their doctor's surgery in Sligo to allow blood samples to be taken from them so that their DNA profiles could be extracted and compared to any DNA that might be present in the remains.

During the search, a forensic anthropologist, Laureen Buckley, had received a call from Detective Inspector John O'Reilly asking her to look at the items that gardaí had recovered. On 14 February, she had gone to the City Morgue to conduct an examination. She had continued her work in the following days and, again, in March, after more bones had been found. She was able to say that the bones that had been found along the shore of Lough Gill were human.

She told the Central Criminal Court that 65 per cent of a human skeleton had been recovered. From the colour, texture and size, all of the bones appeared to have come from the same person: a female aged between 14 and 16 years at the time of her death. The bones had been subjected to the elements and to animals. There was evidence of bite marks and shearing of the bones which was attributable to animals. No facial bones had been found but the skull was present, although eroded and decayed. Ms Buckley said that skull bones in a human fuse at the age of 18. That process had not occurred with this skull, so she was able to say that the person was under that age. It was not possible to establish the height of the person because the skeleton was incomplete.

Her examination of the vertebrae had also indicated that the remains had belonged to a young person. The vertebrae had suffered significant post-mortem damage and the ribs had been severely chewed by animals. Ms Buckley told the court that animals will attack the side of the body to get a bite. The bones in the forearm and the thigh and calf were present but had been nibbled and scratched by rodents.

The jury heard that the pelvis of a child is in three parts that fuse at puberty. The pelvis that had been found had completely fused which, therefore, indicated that the person had reached that stage in life. The skeleton had been identifiable as female because of the size of the pelvis.

Ms Buckley was of the opinion that the remains were in a very advanced state of decay for a person who had been missing for a maximum of 17 months. The body must have been buffeted against the rocks. The skull was likely to have fallen from the body and rolled away and parts of it had been dragged away, most likely by foxes and rats. Nothing of the hands or feet had been recovered.

On 14 February, the State Pathologist, Professor Marie Cassidy, had also gone to the City Morgue and had carried out an examination of the, as yet, unidentified remains. In her evidence to the Central Criminal Court, Professor Cassidy explained which parts of the body had been recovered. She said that there had been no soft tissue, muscle, fat or skin left on what had been found of the skeleton. What was left of the skull had shown evidence of being exposed to the elements and it had thinned to an extreme extent. The outside was eroded and the inside was covered in green mildew and moss. Other bones were less weathered. The upper jaw had not been found but the lower jaw was present and contained two teeth. The lower jawbone, or mandible, had thinned but was intact.

Two ribs had been fractured and all of the long bones that had been recovered had been damaged at the ends, which the pathologist believed to be consistent with animal damage. She concluded that the bones had not been in water for the entire period that Melissa had been missing. She believed they had been subjected to animal damage from an early stage. In her opinion, Melissa's clothed body had been removed from the sleeping bag and her remains had then been scattered. The extent and condition of the remains precluded any investigation into a cause of death and it was, therefore, impossible to reach any conclusion at all on that issue.

Professor Cassidy was asked by Mr Grehan to explain to the jury how a body would react in a strangulation scenario. She said that much depended on the method used. If the neck was compressed, then marks would be visible on the surface of the neck, the face would go very red and haemorrhages would appear in the eyes and skin. Cardiac arrest would result. A victim's reaction would vary greatly depending on the circumstances. A person could suffer immediate cardiac arrest and death. Alternatively, they might struggle for a period of time, perhaps injuring the perpetrator. Some victims may lose consciousness immediately, others may not.

Professor Cassidy could not exclude the possibility of the use of drugs or alcohol or the presence of disease or organ damage.

Mr Justice White asked Professor Cassidy to explain the concept of post-mortem lividity to the jury. She said that, following death, the muscles become floppy and gravity acts upon the blood in the body causing it to drain downwards and pool in the area of the body which is closest to the ground. If a body is lying on its back, the face would appear pale and the back would be discoloured. A tide mark would develop, depending on the position of the body. Mr Justice White mentioned that, during the course of the trial, the jury had heard evidence from Jill that she had seen the deceased in the sleeping bag at the bank of the River Bonet where Jill had said that the body had appeared to be half white and half purple. He asked if this could have been an example of post-mortem lividity. Professor Cassidy said that such an observation would not be unusual.

Mr Grehan questioned the pathologist about how long it would take for lividity to become noticeable. Professor Cassidy said that the process begins immediately upon death and that someone would begin to notice the change in colour after an hour or so. The process could continue for up to 12 hours if the position of the body was altered.

Mr Grehan explained that, in Jill's testimony, Melissa's chest had been moving before she was put into a sleeping bag. She was then put into a car and taken on a 20-minute journey. After only that amount of time, Jill had said she had noticed a discolouration. Professor Cassidy said that would have been a relatively short period of time to show extreme changes and, while the process of lividity would have been ongoing, most people would not notice a colour change that quickly.

Mr Grehan wanted to know if it was possible that an arm around a neck in an apparently friendly gesture could cause death. Professor Cassidy said that it was well recognised that an arm, or arm lock, around the neck could cause sudden death because of the pressure being exerted upon the side of the neck. She said it could happen in a potentially friendly situation as long as pressure was applied to a sensitive area of the neck. Death could, therefore, result without an intention to cause harm.

Professor Cassidy said that if the chest had been seen to be still moving, then it was not a sudden death situation. She agreed that if a neck tie had been placed around the neck, it could obstruct breathing and cause death. She also said that an unconscious person could still make attempts to breathe.

Following her examination of the remains, Professor Cassidy

had contacted dental expert Paul Keogh on 16 February 2008. Mr Keogh is an oral surgeon and a forensic odontologist, meaning he uses dental records to identify human remains. The court heard that there are no formal qualifications for forensic odontology, it is a title bestowed by the State Pathologist's Office. Mr Keogh told the Central Criminal Court that he had worked on hundreds of cases that had required him to identify a person through the examination of dental remains.

He told the court that Professor Cassidy had asked him to come to the City Morgue and examine the jaw bone and teeth that had been recovered at the search site. He explained that it was possible to compile an intricate picture from information gathered from ante-mortem records and compare that picture to the one presented by the remains.

Gardaí had found a lower jaw bone along the shoreline that contained two unerupted wisdom teeth. Another five teeth were found separately.

Melissa's dental records had been retrieved from a dental practice in the United Kingdom. Garda Conway and Detective Scanlon had gone to Mary and Frederick Mahon's home on 12 February 2008 to ask them to sign consent forms to allow gardaí to obtain their daughter's dental records.

Detective Sergeant Con Lee and Detective Garda Pauline McDonagh had travelled to London on 13 February with the forms in their possession. Detective Constable Phil Ellis of New Scotland Yard told the jury that he had collected the detectives from Stansted Airport and, the following day, they had gone to a dental practice in Walthamstow where Melissa had been a patient. There, they had been told that she had undergone treatment in January 2001 at a dental practice in Essex but that the records had been destroyed because of the passage of time. The detectives would have to go to the National Health Service directly. The complete records had eventually been faxed to Sligo Garda Station on 25 February.

Mr Keogh told the court that, from those records, he had been able to tell that Melissa had had fillings in two upper permanent molar teeth. Two of the teeth found by gardaí had had corresponding work done. The two wisdom teeth that were attached to the recovered jaw bone were examined. By looking at the development of those teeth, Mr Keogh was able to tell the that remains belonged to a teenager aged between 14 and 17 years. The dental practice that Melissa had attended in England had taken a radiograph of her jaw. That x-ray and the recovered wisdom teeth were compared and found to be very similar. Mr Keogh was also able to determine, from the fact that the dental arch was intact, that all teeth were present at the time of death.

Mr Keogh was satisfied that the ante-mortem record reconciled with the post-mortem remains in that there were no inconsistencies or contradictions between the material found and the dental records. He told the Central Criminal Court that, in his opinion, the remains were those of Melissa Mahon. There were degrees of identification and while a full set of recovered teeth gives a higher degree of certainty, it was not essential to recover all teeth before a definite identification could be made. The two fillings documented in Melissa's records had matched the filled teeth that had been found. That match, coupled with the position of the wisdom teeth in the jaw bone, indicated a very high degree of certainty. On 26 February 2008, he had been able to tell Sligo gardaí that he believed the remains were those of Melissa.

Mr Keogh then told the court that he had been asked to remove one tooth from the jaw bone that would later be used to extract a DNA profile. The tooth was sent to the United Kingdom Forensic Science Service in Birmingham where technology existed that was used in cases where there was potentially very little usable material available.

A standard test may have produced a result but the technology available in Birmingham enabled a 'low grade' sample to be used. Environmental factors could have degraded the tooth and the DNA it contained. Bacterial activity in a moist and damp area could have led to rapid decay. Cold water, however, would have slowed the decaying process. A tooth had been chosen rather than a piece of bone because it was more intact than, for example, the skull, and the tooth's enamel casing would have protected the material within. If the tooth had been badly degraded, then scientists would not have been able to extract a DNA profile at all.

The molar was dirty and pale green in colour but was unbroken so there was a sufficient amount of material available to enable the British scientists to carry out the process which would allow a DNA profile to be extracted. The tooth was cleaned with a chemical solution to remove impurities and then ground down into a fine powder. That powder was then washed to bring out the DNA which was then suspended in a purified solution. Results were generated by computer and compared to DNA extracted from the blood samples taken from Mary and Frederick Mahon.

Valerie Tomlinson travelled from Birmingham to tell the court that the DNA from the blood samples was examined to see if the molar tooth came from a person who was the natural daughter of Frederick and Mary. It was found that the results were in keeping with that being the case and, statistically speaking, it was 200 million times more likely that the tooth came from their natural daughter than from a person unrelated to them.

A number of other scientists from England were brought to Dublin for the trial to give detailed evidence about the transportation of the blood samples and the tooth. Each person who had custody of the samples or who had worked with them had to tell the court what role they had played. This had to be done to establish the chain of evidence and to prove the results that had been presented in court.

The prosecution had been put on strict proof of even this aspect of the case but the defence ultimately made no issue about the identity of the remains found at Lough Gill and accepted that they belonged to Melissa Mahon.

14 | THE CLOSING STAGES

The prosecution case drew to close after 21 days of evidence. Ms Kennedy told the court that the State had completed its evidence and Mr Grehan indicated that he had an application to make in the absence of the jury.

At this stage of a criminal trial, the defence can ask the trial judge to withdraw the case from the jury's consideration and direct it to find the accused not guilty of any or all charges on the basis that the prosecution had not presented a case that could result in a conviction.

The test used by the courts in this application had been set out in the *Galbraith* case. Mere inconsistencies in the prosecution case will not result in a direction of no case to answer. Only if those inconsistencies are such as to render it unfair to proceed with the trial would a judge exercise his discretion to direct an acquittal. Where a judge concludes that the prosecution case is such that a properly directed jury could not convict upon it, such a direction may also be given.

If weaknesses in the prosecution case had arisen from the view taken of a witness's reliability, then the matter should be left within the province of the jury. Where, on one possible view of the facts, there has been evidence upon which a jury could properly come to the conclusion that the accused is guilty, then it is for the jury to try the matter.

The judge must not usurp the function of the jury. The trial judge has the final word in all matters of law in a case, but the jury members are the sole deciders of the facts.

Mr Grehan told the court that the State had presented evidence that Melissa Mahon's remains had been recovered adjacent to an area in which his client's daughters had said Melissa had been placed. Beyond that, he said, the evidence was that the accused had known Melissa, that she had been a regular visitor to his house and that she had spent a number of weeks in his house in August 2006 and during the time when she had been in residential care in Lis na nÓg. He said that evidence had been adduced that there was extensive contact between the mobile phones which had been attributed to Melissa Mahon and Ronnie Dunbar.

There had been a suggestion of an 'inappropriate sexual relationship' between his client and Melissa but Ronnie Dunbar had denied any such relationship. He also denied any allegation that he had had anything to do with the killing of Melissa Mahon or that he had had any part to play in placing her body into the River Bonet.

Mr Grehan reminded the court that there was no charge before the court that alleged an inappropriate relationship. He accepted that there had been various pieces of evidence that might suggest such an involvement but said that some of that evidence had been 'thoroughly discredited'.

He said the case hinged on the evidence of Dunbar's two daughters. If the jury was to convict his client, it would have to rely on their testimony and find it 'credible, believable and reliable'. Mr Grehan said this posed a 'major problem' for the prosecution case.

He described the evidence given by Angelique Sheridan that the accused had said he would not go to prison for Melissa and would strangle her first as 'very frail and tenuous'. He said Angelique Sheridan had made a number of statements to gardaí in September 2006 but, although she had a lot to say about

Dunbar, all of it negative, she had not made any reference to this threat. She had told no one that he had threatened to kill the girl until after he had been nominated in public as the person who had murdered Melissa Mahon.

Shirley Dunbar had been instrumental in getting Samantha to contact gardaí and had given evidence for the prosecution, yet she had had no recollection of any comment of this kind ever having been made. Mr Grehan said that Angelique Sheridan's evidence was 'extremely tenuous in nature'.

He continued, saying that the difficulty with the evidence of Samantha and her sister was that their accounts differed. 'They did not add up. They did not gel,' he said. Samantha had been quite adamant that all she had seen in the bedroom was her father's right arm around Melissa Mahon's neck. Her impression had been that it was simply a hug. She had also been adamant that her sister was in the room at the time. Mr Grehan accepted that there was 'some agreement' between the sisters but there were also glaring differences. Jill had said that her father had strangled Melissa with a tie and with his bare hands and had also used a pillow to smother her.

'I say Jill's account is incredible in itself,' he said.

She had given several different accounts up to July 2008 and had then, at the last minute, following cross-examination, had added testimony about her father choking Melissa with his hands.

'These are two wildly inconsistent accounts of Melissa Mahon's death from the only two witnesses who claim they were there when it happened.'

At this stage of the application, Mr Justice White said he had no hesitation in saying that Jill was an unreliable witness in the eyes of the law but, he said, conclusions could be drawn from the manner of the disposal of the body.

Mr Grehan said that conclusions in relation to an unlawful killing might be drawn from the method of disposal but it was 'wholly unsuitable' to leave the jury to decide between two 'gravely differing' accounts. Other than those statements, he said, there was not enough evidence to go to the jury.

In order to convict someone of murder, the jury must find an intention to kill or cause serious harm, and such intention, although present in Jill's account, was absent from Samantha's evidence. Mr Grehan said that the prosecution's best case could only be one of manslaughter.

Mr Grehan submitted that the second charge against Dunbar, of threatening to kill Samantha, had not been 'amplified' in Samantha's evidence. At most Samantha's evidence had been that her father had told her that he would do to her what he had done to Melissa.

Ms Kennedy responded to the defence's application by saying that there was 'ample' evidence to enable the jury to make a decision about the accused man's guilt or innocence. She said the intention required to convict of murder could be inferred from the evidence. Difficulties with the testimonies given by the daughters had to be seen in light of their young ages at the time of Melissa's death and the terror in which they held their father. The court had heard about the level of control Dunbar exerted over his daughters and over other witnesses in the case.

Counsel for the prosecution said that a core issue in relation to the killing had been the location of the disposal of Melissa's body. She also said that the evidence given by the State Pathologist about how a person may react in the circumstances described by Samantha, fitted with the testimony given.

Mr Justice White said, 'I am satisfied that it would be wrong to withdraw the case from the jury.'

Mr Justice White then continued, saying that he would leave the case to the jury and, in doing so, was looking at the evidence as a whole. He said that it seemed to have been conceded by Mr Grehan that the skeletal remains found at the shore of Lough Gill were those of Melissa Mahon. He said the jury was entitled to draw that same conclusion in relation to the remains based on the detailed forensic evidence that had been presented by the prosecution.

He said that the jury was also entitled to conclude that Melissa had died at the hands of the accused and, based on the evidence given by Samantha and her younger sister, that it had not been an accident. There were inconsistencies in the evidence given by the two sisters but, he said, 'It is for the jury to evaluate and determine their credibility and accept or reject all or parts of their evidence. There are certain customs and traditions associated with death in this country,' he added, 'One does not normally dispose of a body as one might dispose of a dog.'

He said the jury was entitled to draw adverse inferences from the manner of the disposal of the body and have regard to the subsequent conduct of the accused man. In particular, the jury could take into account the claims Dunbar had made during interview when under arrest and detained in Sligo Garda Station that he had had no contact with Melissa after she had run away from the foster home in Kinlough. The accused man's mobile phone had made contact with Melissa Mahon's phone on the morning of 14 September and a conversation had taken place which, according to phone records, lasted for over eight minutes. Regard should also be given to the pretence made by the accused that Melissa was still alive after September 2006.

'I do not consider any inconsistency in the prosecution case to be so great that the case cannot properly go to the jury,' he said.

If the jury was satisfied that Melissa had died as the result of an unlawful killing, then it could at least convict the accused of manslaughter. If it is satisfied that an intention to kill existed, then it was open to the jury to convict of murder.

'It would be wholly wrong if I was to withdraw the case from the jury at this stage of the trial. I would be the laughing stock of the judiciary, the legal profession and the public at large if I was to withdraw this case and such an action would provide justifiable cause for my resignation or impeachment.'

Mr Grehan's application had failed. He indicated to the court that the defence would not be presenting any evidence. It was time for closing speeches by the prosecution and the defence which would be followed by the judge's charge before the jury was sent out to begin its deliberations. The defence, it should be remembered, is not in any way obligated to 'go into evidence'. The burden of proof lies with the prosecution and remains with the prosecution throughout the trial.

The following morning, Ms Kennedy addressed the members of jury. She told them that they should apply their common sense to the case and to the evidence. If they did so, they would find that the accused had killed Melissa Mahon and, when he did so, he had intended to kill her or cause her serious injury. Ms Kennedy then highlighted certain aspects of the prosecution's case and reviewed the evidence about how Melissa had come to live in Sligo with her parents and how she had become involved with the Dunbar family. She took the jury again through the events of the summer of 2006 when Melissa had first gone missing from her family home and had spent increasing amounts of time with the accused before going into the care of the Health Service Executive.

Ms Kennedy reminded the jury that it had heard evidence that there had been a relationship between the 14-year-old girl and the now 44-year-old man, and evidence of a 'level of control' by the accused over his daughters, Melissa and employees of the Health Service Executive.

She reviewed the evidence of Catherine Farrelly that, on 24 August 2006, the accused had facilitated a meeting between the social worker and Melissa. The accused had called Catherine Farrelly and had told her that Melissa had contacted him and had agreed to meet on certain conditions stipulated by the teenager. Ms Farrelly had told the court that while she had been in the accused's car on the way to Slish Wood, he had received a phone call and had said it was Melissa. Detective Garda William O'Neill had told the court that phone records indicated that, at the time of that call, Angelique Sheridan had actually telephoned Ronnie Dunbar. Angelique Sheridan had told the jury that she had agreed to take Melissa to the meeting place and remain out of sight.

'He was a man in a position of control. He controlled these women. They did what he wanted them to do,' said Ms Kennedy.

She said that Samantha and her sister were frightened of their father. The youngest girl had provided a number of different statements in an attempt to prevent him from getting into trouble. She wanted to protect him. He had threatened to kill himself and, during a search of the accused's house, gardaí had found the very means he had threatened to use, caustic soda and a syringe.

The jury had heard evidence of a relationship between Melissa and the accused. Her sister, Leeanna Mahon, had seen them lying together on a sofa with Melissa between his legs with her head on his chest. The youngest Dunbar girl had seen her father lying on top of Melissa on his bed on the day that Melissa had died. She had testified that her father had said he was keeping Melissa 'sweet'. Samantha had had a conversation with Melissa in which the girl had admitted to a sexual relationship with the accused, which he had then confirmed to Samantha.

Ms Kennedy asked the jury to consider the level of telephone contact between the accused and Melissa. Over 30 per cent of his phone usage involved contact with the 14 year old and, following that very high level of contact, calls from his phone to her phone stopped completely after 19 September 2006.

Both the accused's daughters had said that Melissa and their father had been lying side by side on the bed with his arm around her neck. Both had said she had been wearing black tracksuit bottoms and a Beauty and the Beast nightdress. Ms Kennedy acknowledged that the girls differed in certain respects but, she said, 'We are dealing with two young girls who were under the control of their father and they were frightened by him. The core of the evidence is for you to consider.'

Ms Kennedy told the jury that there was 'ample' evidence to support the prosecution's contention that Ronald Dunbar had murdered Melissa Mahon and had threatened to kill his daughter, Samantha.

Brendan Grehan had spent 20 days cross-examining the State's witnesses and it was now time for him to make his closing speech to the jury.

He began by saying, 'There are serious difficulties with the prosecution case and with Ms Kennedy's conclusion that there is ample evidence to support the prosecution contention that Ronald Dunbar is guilty. This is a case where that is clearly not so. I ask you to decide this case on the evidence. If ever there was a case where an awful lot of prejudice and emotional baggage was present, this is one such matter.'

Mr Grehan tackled one of his biggest problems head on. Dunbar looked guilty. Mr Grehan bluntly acknowledged that his client was not a man who drew sympathy or understanding from those who had come into contact with him, or had watched him in court or had seen him on the news. There was a feeling in this case that one could just tell that Ronnie Dunbar was guilty.

Members of the defence team had advised Dunbar to wear appropriate clothing for court but, always his own man, he had ignored their sartorial advice. He had arrived in court each day wearing tracksuit bottoms and a tight black or grey, short-sleeved T-shirt. His many tattoos were on clear display. He was not going to hide behind a well-dressed veneer.

'He presents as he is. What he is and what you see is someone who is heavily tattooed and muscular in build,' said Mr Grehan.

Counsel acknowledged that his client appeared to be a man who was, 'belligerent, anti-authority and someone who refused to 'kowtow' in a way that others might'.

Mr Grehan said that Dunbar obviously harboured what everyone could agree were 'strange' beliefs that a new world order was coming and that, when that day came, he would lead his army in battle. He thought he could fight demons. Dunbar was a difficult and awkward person who wanted always to control the situations in which he found himself. He was also somebody with a deep-seated difficulty with the gardaí and the manner in which he perceived the investigation into Melissa's death had been conducted. Dunbar felt that he had been hung out to dry, hounded by the media and demonised. He had used every opportunity to criticise gardaí and social workers who had been involved with Melissa.

'He may not be someone to your liking,' said Mr Grehan, 'but do not judge a book by its cover. Do not make a leap, because of those matters, to finding him guilty of murder.'

Counsel said that the people in court and in the media held a shared opinion, that Dunbar must be guilty of murder. Mr Grehan told the jury that it may well feel that his client was guilty of other crimes, with which he had not been charged, in relation to the sexual abuse of Melissa Mahon or the manner by which her body had been disposed of, but that did not render him guilty of the crimes of which he was actually accused.

Mr Grehan suggested that Ms Kennedy had abandoned to some extent the evidence of the youngest Dunbar sister. He said the prosecution had opened and closed the case based on Samantha's account and was entreating the jury to rely upon it entirely.

'You cannot do justice if you simply mix and match the accounts,' he said.

He told the jury members that it was not possible to discard Jill's evidence where they did not believe her and then hold on to some of her evidence in order to support or bolster Samantha's account.

'You have an incredible division between the core evidence of Jill and Samantha. Even now you have not heard the truth after five weeks. The accounts that have been given are radically inconsistent and inherently incredible. They simply have not told you the truth.'

Mr Grehan said that he was conscious that neither had his client told the jury what had happened. Dunbar had, from the beginning, taken the position that he was not going to comment at all on what his daughters said about Melissa's death. Mr Grehan told the jury that an accused person in a criminal trial is entitled to sit back, make no contribution and let the State prove its case against him if it could.

'We have offered no explanation, nor are we obliged to,' said Mr Grehan.

He told the jury that it could not speculate about the dysfunctional nature of his client's family. 'Suffice to say, he is entitled to take the position that he has taken.' The case, Mr Grehan argued, had to rest on the accounts given by Samantha and Jill who were direct eye witnesses to what they said had occurred.

Mr Grehan then turned to the evidence given by Angelique Sheridan. He noted that Ms Kennedy had conceded that Dunbar's daughter, Shirley, had told the court that she did not recall the conversation during which Angelique had said his client

had revealed a plan to murder Melissa rather than go to jail for
her. 'Why', asked Mr Grehan, 'if this threat had been made did Ms
Sheridan not provide that information to the authorities? Her
excuse had been that she was frightened.' Mr Grehan said it was
'incredible' that she had told gardaí about such a conversation in
circumstances where gardaí were conducting an investigation
into Melissa's disappearance. Mr Grehan said that Angelique had
had little difficulty in saying 'other things' to gardaí about his
client. The exact contents of her pre-trial statements were not
disclosed to the jury, but Mr Grehan had, during the cross-
examination of gardaí, established that she had said many
unflattering things about her former boyfriend.

Also, Mr Grehan continued, if Jill had told Angelique that
Melissa was three months pregnant, why had she not shared this
crucial information with gardaí? He said that there had been no
suggestion during Jill's evidence that she had known that Melissa
was pregnant or had ever said anything of that nature to
Angelique. In 2007, Angelique had made a statement to gardaí in
relation to this case that had run to two and a half pages and still
had not mentioned the threat to kill Melissa or that the teenager
was pregnant. It was not until the story broke in the media that
Melissa's remains had been found that Angelique broke her
silence.

'You couldn't hang a dog on that kind of evidence,' said Mr
Grehan.

Mr Grehan had accepted in the absence of the jury during his
application to withdraw the case from it that the remains found
at Lough Gill were Melissa Mahon's. He now made that
concession in front of the jury, after requiring the prosecution to
prove that by forensic evidence and dental records.

'You will have little difficulty in concluding that the remains
found were Melissa's,' he said.

He also said that the members of the jury may well reach a
conclusion about how Melissa's body had got into the water and
whether or not his client had been involved, but he cautioned
them not to then make the leap to finding him guilty of murder.

The accounts of the daughters had varied and even if they

were 15 and 13 years old at the time and still quite young, Samantha had 'already at that stage perhaps done a lot more living than most teenagers'. Mr Grehan said she had used drugs, been in various types of trouble and had left school and, instead, had been attending the Youth Reach programme. She had had difficulties with her father who had thrown her out of the house. She had ended up living rough and had been taken into the care of the Health Service Executive in late 2007. Mr Grehan said that the prosecution had painted a picture in which his client's daughters were under his control but they clearly, in his submission, were not. Samantha, he said, was not really under any control.

Simple matters had curiously failed to add up. When questioned about where she had slept, Samantha had given confused and contradictory answers and had told a peculiar story of moving rooms in the middle of the night. Mr Grehan told the jury that he did not 'have a clue' what had gone on during that exchange in his cross-examination of Samantha.

He listed the differences between the accounts. Samantha had insisted that the front door had been unlocked and she had let herself in. Jill had remembered Samantha knocking on a door before she had let her in. Samantha had said her sister was crying; Jill had denied that that was the case. Samantha had said Jill had told her not to go upstairs; Jill had told the court that she had told Samantha the opposite. Samantha's evidence had been that her father had jumped away from Melissa on the bed; whereas Jill had said that he had continued to lie beside the girl. Crucially, Jill had told the court that her father had put a neck tie around Melissa's neck; Samantha had said that had never happened.

Samantha's account had included her attempting to resuscitate Melissa but Jill had made no mention of this. Jill had said she had been holding the tie around Melissa's neck for two or three minutes before she had remembered to go downstairs and turn off the oven. Jill had also said that her father had put a pillow over Melissa's face and had smothered her. She had then chosen her re-examination by Ms Kennedy to mention, for the first time, that the accused had leaned over the bed, put two hands around

Melissa's neck and strangled her. Samantha, on the other hand, had said she did not see any violence being done to Melissa.

At the bank of the River Bonet, Jill had said that her father had opened the sleeping bag into which he had placed Melissa's body and had removed the tie from around her neck. Samantha had said this did not happen. Samantha had also told the jury that she had not gone to Youth Reach the following day because she had been too upset, but the attendance records from the programme indicated that she had been present every day up until 29 September 2006.

'Neither account is consistent with the other. Neither account is inherently credible.'

Mr Grehan continued, telling the court that Jill had variously said that Samantha had killed Melissa, that her father had done it and that all three of them had done it. She had claimed that the accused had brainwashed her into giving these accounts. As a result, said Mr Grehan, the prosecution had 'nailed its colours' to Samantha's account. He said he had great concerns in relation to the suggestion that the arm around Melissa's neck that Samantha had described could so easily lead to an inference that his client had strangled her. Mr Grehan had asked Samantha exactly what she had seen and what she had described had not included violence. Mr Grehan said that there did not seem to be a suggestion that Dunbar had done anything to Melissa's neck, it had looked like he was giving her a hug. Mr Grehan reminded the jury that Samantha had said she had not been there when it had started and said it was clear that she was not describing a 'choke hold'. Samantha had no evidence to offer about what had gone on before she had entered the room.

'Neither of my client's two daughters came across as in any way shrinking violets or girls who would be pushed into doing anything,' said Mr Grehan.

Mr Grehan described the evidence offered about a sexual relationship between Melissa and his client as 'very scant indeed'. Samantha had suggested that her father had made admissions to her. Leeanna Mahon had told the court that she had seen her sister on the sofa with Dunbar, as had Jill. That had been the 'beginning and end' of the evidence. Jill had said she had seen her father on a bed, fully clothed, with Melissa 10 minutes before she had said he killed her. Mr Grehan told the jury that it might have its suspicions having heard evidence that Melissa had taken a pregnancy test that was positive. He warned that it certainly had not been said by the witnesses that Dunbar was the father and there had been some suggestion that Melissa had been seeing someone else at the time.

He said Samantha's account simply did not add up. It was like a silent movie, actions but no words spoken, nothing said by her father. Confronted with the situation that Samantha had said she had walked into, surely she would have asked what was going on. By her account, she had said nothing.

Professor Cassidy had told the court that compression of the neck could immediately cause cardiac arrest and death. According to Samantha, however, Melissa had still been breathing after Dunbar had got off the bed, which was not consistent with an immediate death. Mr Grehan suggested that the instinctive reaction to being strangled would be to try to remove whatever is restricting the throat. Samantha's story did not add up.

'You can't simply pick and mix pieces of evidence. You have to rely full square on Samantha's evidence and it does not come up to the threshold needed for murder,' concluded Mr Grehan.

When the prosecution and defence have made their closing speeches, it is the role of the trial judge to charge the jury. This involves the judge reviewing the evidence, drawing attention to its salient parts and instructing the jury about what the law is and how it should be applied in the particular case under consideration.

Mr Justice White told the jury that the State must prove that Melissa Mahon was dead and that she had been killed unlawfully. The State must then satisfy the jury, beyond a reasonable doubt, that Ronald Dunbar had killed her or had acted in concert with another person in the pursuit of a joint plan to kill her. The concept of joint enterprise or common design provides that parties who enter into an agreement to commit an offence are each as liable for it as the other.

If the jury was satisfied that Dunbar had killed Melissa, then it must at least find him guilty of manslaughter. If it was satisfied that he had intended to kill her, then it must convict of murder. Mr Justice White said that the defence now seemed not to be contesting that the remains found were those of Melissa Mahon. He also repeated the remark that he had made during the defence application to withdraw the case from the jury that there were certain customs and traditions associated with death. 'One does not just dump a deceased in the river.'

Mr Justice White went through the evidence that had been given by Samantha, Jill and Angelique on the same day that the jury had heard the closing speeches by counsel. It was Thursday, 21 May 2008, the 22nd day of the trial. The Central Criminal Court did not sit the following day because of a judges conference and Mr Justice White held over the remainder of his charge until the following Monday morning.

On that Monday, he told the jury to leave aside any sense of revulsion or sympathy it may have and treat the case in a clinical and dispassionate manner. It was for the jury to assess the credibility of witnesses. The ages of Samantha and Jill and the evidence of Jill in light of her previous accounts were also matters for its consideration.

According to Samantha and Jill, the accused had told his daughters that they were accomplices to murder. Mr Justice White said that if it was the case that the girls had assisted their father in the disposal of Melissa's body, then in the eyes of the law they were accomplices as accessories after the fact. He warned the jury that it was dangerous to convict an accused based on the uncorroborated evidence of accomplices. He also said it was a matter for the jury as to whether it had heard evidence which was capable of amounting to corroboration. It could still, however, convict in the absence of corroboration if it gave due consideration to his warning.

15 | A SHOCKING END TO A SHOCKING TRIAL

The jury retired to begin its deliberations at 2.45 p.m. on Monday, 25 May—the 23rd day of the trial. The jury was sent home for the evening after two and a half hours and told to return at 10.30 a.m. on Tuesday.

Previously, members of juries, once charged by the trial judge and told to begin their deliberations, were sequestered and had to stay together until they had reached a conclusion. The practice had been to tell a jury near the end of a trial to bring overnight bags and if deliberations ran into a second day, they were brought to a hotel under garda supervision. That requirement was modified in January 2009 to allow judges to use their discretion to let jury members disband at the end of each day and return to their own homes. They are clearly warned throughout the trial and at the start of their deliberations not to discuss the case with anyone, to ignore media coverage and to refrain from discussing the case with each other unless directed to do so by the judge.

Garda Pat Conway had been involved in the case from the very beginning and had attended each day of the trial. After the jury had been sent home for the evening on the first day of its deliberations, prison officers led Dunbar out of the courtroom to the waiting prison van. As he was led through the Round Hall, he spotted Garda Conway, turned his head and said, 'I hope they're paying you overtime for this.' Dunbar spoke with a smile and in a jocular tone. Garda Conway was taken aback and remarked later that it was the first time Dunbar had acknowledged him in the five weeks they had been in court. The garda appeared despondent. He told a reporter that he and Catherine Farrelly had done everything possible to get Melissa back. It had just not been enough to save her.

On Tuesday morning, Mr Justice White sent the jury out at 10.47 a.m. to resume its deliberations. It returned at 12.05 p.m. to ask a question. The foreman of the jury told Mr Justice White that the members wanted to watch Mr Grehan's cross-examination of Samantha again. They particularly wanted to review the section of the evidence where Mr Grehan put Jill's earlier statements to Samantha.

In the ordinary course of events, witnesses cannot be recalled to give their evidence again for the benefit of the jury. In circumstances where a jury want to hear testimony for a second time, the trial judge will read the evidence to the jury from his own note. Samantha, however, had given her evidence via a television link and it had been recorded. The jury now wanted to watch that recording.

Courtroom number two did not have the facility to enable the replaying of recordings, therefore plans were made to move the trial to a suitable courtroom. The jury had made its request at 12.05 p.m. and preparations began at that time.

The jury was not officially deliberating between the time of its request and the following morning because a technical issue arose. The jury was sent to lunch at 12.45 p.m. and at 2 p.m. was brought to courtroom twenty-three within the Four Courts complex where the recording could be viewed.

It is the responsibility of court service technicians to set up television links and record the evidence. At the same time, a transcript of the trial is created by a stenographer from an independent company. Recently, an audio recording system has also been implemented.

After lunch, the jury was shown a section of Samantha's cross-examination for a second time. At the end of the requested portion, the judge asked the foreman if the jury was now satisfied and in a position to resume its deliberations. The foreman indicated that the jury wanted to see a further portion of the recorded evidence. It then emerged that there had been a technical glitch and that the requested evidence could not be found. Mr Justice White expressed his dissatisfaction with the situation but said he had no choice but to let the jury go home for the remainder of the day while court service staff worked to fix the problem.

The following morning, the jury returned to courtroom two and remained in its room while a whisper spread among members of the press that the recording had failed and, as a result, the defence was going to apply to Mr Justice White to discharge the jury. The trial was on the brink of collapse at the final hurdle. If the application succeeded, the entire case would have to be heard again in front of a new jury at a later date.

The basis of the defence application was that section 13 of the 1992 Criminal Evidence Act, which provided for the giving of evidence by underage or vulnerable persons via live television link, stipulated that any such evidence should be video recorded. In this case, a portion of Samantha's evidence had not been recorded. In the absence of the jury, Joseph Barnes BL, the junior counsel for the defence, made the application and argued that as the statutory requirement had not been met, his client had been denied a fair trial. He said that as there was no way to retrospectively fix the mistake, the jury should be discharged.

Mr Justice White was not enthusiastic about the defence position. He said that he had consulted with colleagues overnight and had reached the conclusion that the purpose of the video recording was not to enable a jury to review the evidence but to ensure that a proper record of it had been taken in the event of an appeal to a higher court. He said that a malfunction had occurred but that the evidence had been recorded on the court's audio recording system and he ordered that the audio recording be put on the transcript so that it would be available for appraisal by the

Court of Criminal Appeal in the event of the case coming before that court.

Mr Justice White said that the 1992 Criminal Evidence Act had not given juries the right to see and hear again evidence that had been recorded. He said, 'A jury is entitled to have its memory refreshed from the judge's note or from the transcript. I am not aware of any authority which entitles jurors to seek to have evidence reviewed before them.'

Ms Kennedy signalled that she was in full agreement with Mr Justice White. He then indicated that the audio recording would be played for the jury. He told Mr Barnes, 'Your client has so far received an exceedingly fair trial. I have bent over backwards to accommodate Mr Grehan's cross-examination of witnesses and have given him every latitude.'

The members of the jury were brought into the courtroom at 11.37 a.m. and Mr Justice White explained the situation to them. He said that the equipment had appeared to be recording Samantha's cross-examination but 'for some reason or other' had not done so. He told the jury that the court's independent digital audio recording was available to them and the foreman indicated that the jury would be satisfied to listen to that. Mr Justice White also mentioned to the jury that someone in the media had suggested that the loss of the recording was the fault of the gardaí. He stressed that such a suggestion was entirely inaccurate. The fault was a mechanical one rather than the result of human error and it was court service staff rather than members of the gardaí who had responsibility for the recordings and for the machinery.

When the members of the jury had listened to the requested section of evidence again, they went back to the jury room and resumed their deliberations.

Mr Justice White then asked that he be provided with an explanation for what had gone on. Liam Walsh of the court service took the stand. He said that a hitherto unknown problem with the recording equipment had been discovered and a review of the system would be undertaken as a result. It appeared that if the operator of the equipment completed the start-up procedure too quickly, the machine did not have time to register which channel was being used to record. In this case, the operator had done what he had understood to be correct. A recording light had come on and all had appeared to be in order, but the machine had recorded on the wrong channel and, therefore, did not capture the evidence on the DVD.

As lunch-time approached, Mr Justice White noted that the jury had been out for nearly five and a half hours. It was now appropriate to direct that it could return a majority verdict. At the beginning of deliberations, a jury is told that it must return a unanimous verdict. After a certain period of time, usually over four hours, when it becomes clear that the jury has not been able to reach such a verdict, it is told that it may return a verdict upon which at least 10 of its number are agreed.

When members of the Dunbar jury were brought out of their room to be sent to lunch, the foreman confirmed that they had not yet reached a unanimous verdict. He was told that, after the break, they would be directed in relation to a majority verdict. During lunch, or any other breaks, the jury is prohibited from continuing its deliberations.

Everyone dispersed. The jury members were taken to lunch by the garda who had charge of them and returned to their room at 2 p.m. A few minutes later, the court room filled again. Everyone was expecting to hear a majority direction but before Mr Justice White had returned to the courtroom, a knock came from inside the door of the jury room. There was a verdict.

Surprise spread throughout the courtroom. Lawyers, the Mahon family, the press, investigating gardaí and Ronnie Dunbar waited for the judge to take his position. The jury was brought out and the registrar asked the foreman if the jury had reached a decision on which all of its members were agreed. He replied that it had. The jury had gone from indecision before the lunch break to unanimous agreement after it.

There is no way of knowing how this situation arose. Technically, the jury should have waited until it was officially sent back to its deliberations.

The issue paper on which both charges and the verdicts against Dunbar were recorded was handed to the registrar. The verdicts were read aloud. On the first count, of the murder of Melissa Mahon, the jury had found Ronnie Dunbar not guilty of murder but guilty of manslaughter. On the second count of threatening to kill Samantha Dunbar, the jury found him not guilty.

The verdict was met with stunned silence. Dunbar did not react. Mr Justice White thanked the members of jury and said that he was certain that they had found the case difficult to determine. 'This has been a distasteful, sordid and squalid case and I discharge you from further jury service for the rest of your lives,' he said.

Mr Grehan told the court that the defence had been instructed by Dunbar not to seek to have any reports compiled on his behalf. Neither would the defence call any evidence in mitigation and so the judge was in a position to proceed to sentence immediately.

Mr Justice White said that he was not in a position to sentence Dunbar there and then. He required assistance from the Director of Public Prosecutions about manslaughter sentences in similar cases that had involved the killing of a 14-year-old child. Mr Grehan suggested to the court that his client's case should now be viewed as involuntary manslaughter as the jury's verdict had indicated that the intention to kill or cause serious harm was absent. Mr Justice White replied that what the jury's verdict actually indicated was that it was not satisfied beyond a reasonable doubt that the intention was present.

Dunbar was remanded in custody until his sentence date of 6 July 2009.

The Mahon family left the Four Courts without speaking to the media.

Those who had followed the trial closely from day one were left dumbfounded. A murder conviction had largely been expected, even taking the conflicting elements of the accused daughters' testimonies into account. The gardaí involved in the case appeared to be relieved that Dunbar had at least been convicted of manslaughter and had not walked free. The detectives, even after the sentencing, remained tight-lipped on their opinions about what had occurred.

The mandatory sentence for murder is life and when such a

verdict is delivered, the accused is sentenced on the spot because there is no need to review relevant case law or hear pleas in mitigation. The sentence for manslaughter is discretionary and Mr Justice White was at large to impose as short or as long a sentence as he saw fit. There was a feeling that the judge would be reluctant to deal lightly with Ronnie Dunbar.

Dunbar's face appeared on the front pages of most of the national newspapers the following day. During the course of a trial, the media must be careful not to prejudice the jury and, for the previous five weeks, the papers had published only a contemporaneous report of what had gone on in the courtroom. After the verdict had been announced, the revulsion caused by the case was palpable. Dunbar was called a beast, a paedophile and a brute. The juxtaposition of the reports of the verdict which confirmed that Dunbar was a child killer and Ruth Nooney's declarations of undying love served to underline the bizarre and twisted nature of the case.

Shirley Dunbar again spoke to the *Sunday World* and expressed her disgust with the verdict. She could not understand how her father had only been convicted of manslaughter and felt that Melissa had not received the justice she deserved. She said that, from day one, her father had tried to blame Samantha for Melissa's death and, while she still had feelings for him, she had wanted to see him convicted of murder and imprisoned for the rest of his life. She also attacked the Health Service Executive saying that social workers had not done enough to protect Melissa, who had clearly been infatuated with Dunbar. Shirley said her father was a paedophile and yet, while social workers noted the infatuation, they placed Melissa in a residential unit which was only streets away from him.

As soon as the verdict was announced, the Health Service Executive released the following statement:

> The HSE wishes to express its deepest sympathy to the family and friends of the late Melissa Mahon. Social work and support staff from the time of referral were intensely involved with Melissa for a period of seven months, from February to

September 2006. A case management review as part of routine procedure and provided for under the Children First National Guidelines for the Protection and Welfare of Children 1999 will now be carried out. The HSE was precluded from commencing this review until the legal proceedings surrounding this case were completed.

16 | SENTENCING

On the morning of Monday, 6 July 2009, the participants in the trial reconvened at courtroom number two in the Round Hall of the Four Courts. The Mahon family, including Mary, Frederick and 11 others, arrived and filed into their seats at 10.45 a.m. The press were, as usual, out in force and a rumour was spreading among reporters that the Mahon family would not speak to the media outside the court. The common practice is that members of the bereaved family give their reaction to the sentence outside the public entrance of the Four Courts in front of all media representatives. The word was that the Mahons, instead, had made a deal with the *News of the World* and would talk to that paper exclusively.

At 11.05 a.m., prison officers marched Dunbar into the courtroom and up to his regular seat in the bench near his defence team at the left-hand side of the court. He had eschewed his tight, short-sleeved T-shirts for a long sleeved, navy sports top, hiding, for once, his heavily tattooed arms. He wore black tracksuit bottoms and carried a black jacket. He had also shaved his head and beard completely. In the 15 minutes before Mr Justice White entered the room, Dunbar read from papers he held out of sight under the ledge of his bench. Even at this late stage of the trial process, he could not be passive.

After the arrival of Mr Justice White at 11.20 a.m., Ms Kennedy began to summarise the facts of the case for the trial judge. She explained the circumstances that had brought Dunbar and his daughters to Sligo, and to Rathbraughan Park, and briefly outlined how his daughters had come into contact with Melissa Mahon. It had been 39 days since Dunbar had been convicted of manslaughter and the facts were obviously still fresh in the minds of everyone involved, however the prosecution is obliged at sentencing to refresh the court's memory and put certain matters on the record.

Ms Kennedy mentioned that Melissa had gone missing on a number of occasions. She had been reported missing on 4 August 2006, entered residential care on 28 August 2006 and was last seen on 14 September 2006. She explained that Melissa's remains had been found on 11 February 2008. As Ms Kennedy delved more deeply into a summary of the evidence given during the trial, the defence began to raise objections. Ms Kennedy explained that Samantha and her younger sister had given evidence via video link over a number of days. She told the court that Samantha had said that her father had orchestrated the meeting between Melissa and Catherine Farrelly at Slish Wood. Ms Kennedy repeated Samantha's evidence about how she had come home from Youth Reach to find her sister upset and crying and had gone upstairs to find her father lying side by side on a bed with Melissa with his arm around her neck. Counsel then turned to the youngest girl's evidence that Dunbar had strangled Melissa. At this point, Mr Grehan got to his feet and objected to the giving of that evidence on the basis that it did not accord with the jury's finding of manslaughter.

Mr Justice White permitted the prosecution to continue, saying that the Court of Criminal Appeal was entitled to have all matters put on the transcript. Ms Kennedy went on to repeat Jill's evidence that she had seen her father use a tie around Melissa's neck, strangle her with his bare hands and place a pillow over her face to smother her.

Ms Kennedy reviewed the facts of the disposal of Melissa's body, describing how the then 15-year-old Samantha and her then

13-year-old sister had got into their father's car with him, having put Melissa's body in the boot, and travelled to the River Bonet where Samantha had helped her father to throw Melissa into the water.

Detective Inspector John O'Reilly took the stand and agreed with Ms Kennedy that her synopsis of events had been accurate. He then went through the story once again in greater detail. He explained that Melissa had been in the care of the Health Service Executive under an Emergency Care Order made on 28 August 2006. He talked about the District Court Order of 7 September 2006 that had prohibited Dunbar from having contact with Melissa without the prior consent of her social workers and how that turn of events had left her 'quietly upset'. He said that she had been placed in a foster home in Kinlough, County Leitrim, the night before her disappearance but had run away and was picked up by gardaí and her social worker. He explained how, the next morning, Catherine Farrelly had found Melissa on her mobile talking to what Ms Farrelly could hear was a male voice and how phone records had indicated that Dunbar's phone had called Melissa's phone at that time.

When Detective Inspector O'Reilly and Ms Kennedy entered into the area of the nature of Melissa's relationship with Dunbar, Mr Grehan again got to his feet to raise an objection. Mr Justice White permitted the repetition of Samantha's evidence that Melissa had told Samantha, in a conversation overheard by Dunbar, that she was in love with her father and was having a sexual relationship with him. Mr Justice White also listened again to the evidence that Dunbar had entered the living room during the conversation and had admitted to Samantha that what Melissa had said was true. The judge reheard the evidence given by Angelique Sheridan that Dunbar had said he would not go to prison for Melissa and would strangle the teenager before he would allow that to happen.

Detective Inspector O'Reilly and Ms Kennedy brought the court through a summary of Samantha's and her younger sister's evidence about what had happened the day they had found their father in bed with Melissa and the steps that had been taken to recover her body in February 2008, after Samantha made her first statement to gardaí.

The sentence hearing had so far run its course in a similar manner to any other hearing of its kind. Ms Kennedy, having refreshed the court's memory in relation to the evidence heard during the trial, then turned her attention to the effect the crime had had on the Mahon family. To that end, she told the court that she would read a victim impact statement prepared by Mary Mahon on behalf of the Mahon family. At this point, the hearing took an unprecedented turn. Mr Justice White interrupted counsel and asked to hear evidence of the attitude of the Mahon family towards Melissa's disappearance between the date she had been reported missing and the date on which her remains had been found. Before that evidence was reviewed, Mr Justice White stated that he found a victim impact statement to be disingenuous in the circumstances.

Detective Inspector O'Reilly told the court that, because Melissa had been in the care of the Health Service Executive at the time of her disappearance, the Mahon family had felt that Melissa was the Health Service Executive's responsibility. He said the family adopted that stance for quite some time. They had been asked to make a statement on a number of occasions but only at an advanced stage of the investigation had they felt able to do so. Mr Justice White commented that Mary Mahon had maintained a pretence that Melissa was in England and had told Garda Pat Conway that parties had informed her that her child was in the United Kingdom without ever telling gardaí who those parties were.

Detective Inspector O'Reilly said that Garda Conway had been the family liaison officer and had had a considerable amount of contact with the Mahon family. He said that Garda Conway had had difficulties interacting with Mary Mahon and was only 'drip fed' information. No evidence was ever found that Melissa had been in the UK, despite the fact that searches were carried out there. Garda Conway had had to spend a great deal of time building a relationship with the Mahon family. Detective Inspector O'Reilly said the family had become much more forthcoming after trust had been established.

Mr Justice White asked Ms Kennedy what, in the normal course of events, would be the attitude of a family of a missing person in circumstances similar to this case.

Ms Kennedy replied, 'I think that one could apply one's common sense to answering that question.'

She again turned to the victim impact statement and asked for the court's permission to read it aloud. Mr Justice White said, 'I cannot prevent you from reading it but I find it disingenuous in the extreme.'

Ms Kennedy read to the court the statement Mary Mahon had earlier made to Garda Pat Conway.

> I myself was very depressed from a very early stage. I tried to commit suicide by taking an overdose of tablets. My husband saved me in time. He will not allow tablets in the house now. Leeanna, my second youngest daughter, had been the closest to Melissa and tried to take an overdose a number of times. She also slashed herself on her arms a number of times. She attended Dr Casey for treatment. Yvonne also slashed her arms, but did not attend a doctor. I myself did not attend a doctor. I coped with it in my own way. The whole thing had an emotional effect on my entire family in England and in Ireland. My whole life is gone. She was my baby. My whole life has been torn apart by the loss of our baby Melissa.

Mr Justice White had made his feelings clear about the family's lack of co-operation or assistance with the investigation into Melissa's disappearance. It was an unusual move. The attitude and conduct of a bereaved family rarely attracts negative attention or comment.

The use of a victim impact statement was introduced by section 5 of the Criminal Justice Act 1993 after victim's rights groups campaigned for a voice for victims and their families in the criminal justice system. The section allows judges to hear evidence from the victims of sexual or violent crimes about the impact the offence has had on their lives. A judge is allowed to take such evidence into account in determining an appropriate sentence.

It is not clear from the section what the position is in relation to evidence being taken from those bereaved by the death of a victim of murder or manslaughter. The sentence for murder is mandatory life which leaves the sentencing judge with no discretion and renders the hearing of victim impact evidence irrelevant to the sentence. Judges may feel that the family of the victim is entitled to its day in court and see the statement as a therapeutic tool. Often, the families of murder victims take the opportunity not only to describe the loss they have suffered but also to describe the type of person the victim was before their life was taken from them.

In the case of manslaughter, however, where the maximum sentence is life and the judge has a very wide discretion to impose a sentence he or she thinks suitable, the role of the victim impact statement is somewhat more difficult.

At the sentencing of Wayne O'Donoghue for the manslaughter . of Robert Holohan, the victim's mother sparked controversy when she delivered a provocative victim impact statement that veered away from wording that had been agreed by the defence and prosecution. In her statement, Majella Holohan said that semen had been found on her son's hand although no evidence of such was given during the trial and no sexual motive for the killing of Robert was ever put forward by the prosecution. As a result, the Court of Criminal Appeal warned that the victim impact statement procedure's future could be jeopardised if abused in such a manner.

The *O'Donoghue* case was discussed by counsel for other reasons during Dunbar's sentencing. Mr Grehan sought to draw parallels between the two cases in circumstances where Mr Justice Paul Carney had imposed a four-year sentence on Wayne O'Donoghue. Robert Holohan had been 11 years old when he had been killed by his neighbour. Robert had disappeared from his home in Ballyedmond, near Midleton in County Cork, on 4 January 2005. His body was discovered eight days later, wrapped in black refuse sacks and dumped in a ditch at Inch Strand, about

20 kilometres from his home. Four days later, O'Donoghue confessed to killing the schoolboy. Prior to his confession, O'Donoghue had taken part in the search for Robert and had expressed his concern for the boy to Robert's parents.

Wayne O'Donoghue had killed Robert Holohan by causing him to asphyxiate. He told gardaí that Robert had called to his home on the afternoon of 4 January and had asked him to drive him to McDonald's in Midleton for a milkshake. When O'Donoghue had refused, Robert began throwing stones at his Fiat Punto car. O'Donoghue went over to Robert in the driveway and grabbed the child first with his right hand and then with his left and jerked him away from the car to stop him throwing stones at the vehicle. He then released Robert and the boy fell to the ground. He brought Robert into the bathroom of his home and threw water on his face. When Robert didn't revive, he panicked, got black plastic bags and put them over Robert's head and body. O'Donoghue then carried the body in the bags, put it in the boot of his car and drove down to Ballyedmond, stopping at a local garage to buy a bottle of Lucozade before driving 12 miles to Inch Strand, near Whitegate. There, he threw the child into a ditch and returned later that night with a Coke bottle of petrol to try to burn the plastic he had used to wrap the body.

He was charged with murder but was acquitted by a jury following a 10-day trial. He had pleaded guilty to manslaughter at the outset of the trial, and was jailed for four years by Mr Justice Carney.

Mr Grehan pointed to similarities between the *O'Donoghue* and *Dunbar* cases—an intention to kill or cause serious harm had not been established in either and both defendants had disposed of the bodies and involved themselves in cover-ups that had caused greater distress to the families of the victims. Counsel maintained that there had been no evidence of the infliction of any kind of violence on Melissa Mahon and said that the court had to look at the present case within the parameters of the *O'Donoghue* case. Mr Grehan said Dunbar could not be convicted of manslaughter and sentenced for murder. He also cautioned the court not to sentence Dunbar for any other of the criminal activities that may have been alluded to or alleged against him during the course of the trial.

Ms Kennedy argued that Mr Justice White should not draw parallels with the *O'Donoghue* case. She said that the cases could be distinguished in two ways. Firstly, Wayne O'Donoghue had admitted the killing and shown a high level of remorse and, secondly, he had asserted that the death of Robert Holohan had been an accident. During O'Donoghue's trial, the jury heard that gardaí had found him sitting in an armchair shaking and in a highly distressed state. He told gardaí that he had killed Robert, he said he was a murderer. O'Donoghue had apologised to Robert's family and had taken every opportunity to appear contrite. Dunbar's attitude and behaviour could not be further removed from that of O'Donoghue.

Mr Grehan told the court that it was still unclear to him for what offence precisely his client was to be sentenced. He reminded the court that no positive defence had ever been asserted by Dunbar and if the court was to accept the jury's verdict, then the case must be viewed as one of involuntary manslaughter. Voluntary manslaughter arises in cases where excessive self-defence is used or the accused can demonstrate that they were provoked. Involuntary manslaughter can occur where there had been an assault but an intention to cause serious harm was absent. It also arises in cases where there has been a criminally dangerous or negligent act. Dunbar did not put forward the case that he assaulted Melissa in a minor way, therefore accidentally causing her death, but Mr Grehan seemed to argue that the jury had reached a conclusion of that nature.

As lunch-time approached, Mr Justice White indicated that he needed time to consider Dunbar's sentence and adjourned the case until 10.30 a.m. the following Friday. The Mahon family left the courtroom and, outside the building, made their feelings about the judge's remarks clear to waiting reporters.

Mary Mahon was angry about the unexpected attack on her family from the bench. 'The judge is after having a pop at me, I'm fuming,' she said.

Her husband was asked if the family was angry with Mr Justice

White and said, 'Well, not the judge. It was everyone. The police said it all wrong and everything.'

When Friday, 10 July arrived, the Mahon family decided to stay away from the Four Courts. Only Leeanna Mahon attended, standing at the back of courtroom number two with her boyfriend to hear Dunbar's fate. The court was filled with press and gardaí. Dunbar, dressed in the same casual clothes as he had worn on Monday, strolled in as though he hadn't a care in the world. From his usual seat, he smiled and laughed with his solicitor appearing for all the world like a man who had little, if anything, to worry about.

Mr Justice White entered and asked Dunbar to stand up. He began, 'Melissa Mahon was fourteen years old when she lost her life at your hands. She was a disturbed, fragile and vulnerable child who came from a difficult home and alleged serious abuse.'

The judge was careful to point out that the truth of those allegations could not be established and said that her family was entitled to the presumption of innocence. He said that Melissa had been taken into care but was unsettled there because of her association with Dunbar.

Dunbar had had a detrimental effect on the ability of social workers to interact with Melissa and although a court order was obtained, he nevertheless continued to have close contact with her. Mr Justice White told Dunbar that he had practised deception on social workers by pretending to help them find Melissa while, in fact, he had been harbouring her in his home. The judge said Melissa had become friendly with Dunbar's daughters and had spent a lot of time in his house where, although old enough to be her father, he had preyed on her fragility and vulnerability.

He said there had been evidence during the trial of a sexual relationship and that the court had heard that Melissa had been pregnant. He acknowledged, however, that the allegation that she had been pregnant could not be tested and so Dunbar was entitled to the presumption of innocence.

'After taking Melissa's life, you engaged in a cover-up in which you disposed of the body in a manner not befitting an animal,' he said.

Mr Justice White continued, saying that it had not been possible to establish a cause of death and perhaps it was that lack of information that was foremost in the jury's mind during its deliberations. Dunbar's disposal of Melissa's body was not done in a panic but in a 'calculated and deliberate manner'.

He then addressed Dunbar's conduct during the trial which he had observed closely. Dunbar had come across as 'disdainful, scornful and borderline contemptuous of his surroundings and of the evidence as it was given'. Mr Justice White had no doubt that Mr Grehan had found Dunbar to be a 'most difficult client'. The judge said that he had allowed Mr Grehan an unusual degree of latitude in his cross-examination of witnesses and had risen on a number of occasions before cross-examinations were completed to enable Mr Grehan to take further instructions from his client. Such accommodations were not normally given to counsel with such frequency.

There were no mitigating factors in the case and he had to take into account the evidence that had been given on Monday of Dunbar's previous bad character and criminal convictions from the 1980s and 1990s. Dunbar had offered absolutely no co-operation or assistance. He had not offered a plea of guilty to manslaughter, nor had he offered an apology or shown any degree of remorse.

Mr Justice White then referred to the comments he had made earlier in the week about the Mahon's victim impact statement. He said that the remarks were not directed towards Melissa's siblings and that there had been no suggestion of a lack of co-operation on their part. He accepted and appreciated the effect that their sister's death had had on them. The victim impact report needed to be truthful and reliable evidence of the effect of events on a family in order to enable a judge to properly evaluate the impact of a crime and determine the gravity of the offence and, therefore, the sentence. It was essential that the maker acted in a bona fide manner. Any departure would 'undermine victim impact statements to the detriment of the victims of crime, the common good and the achievement of justice'.

Returning to Dunbar, Mr Justice White reiterated that Mr Grehan had urged the court to consider Dunbar's crime to be at the lower end of the scale of gravity and Ms Kennedy had argued the opposite. A manslaughter conviction gives an extensive discretion to the judge, from a suspended sentence to a life sentence in rare and exceptional circumstances. Mr Justice White said that Ms Kennedy had been correct in her assessment of this case. He could not ignore the evidence adduced during the trial or the fact that the State's opportunity to carry out a meaningful post mortem and establish the cause of death had been frustrated as a direct result of Dunbar's actions. To ignore such would be to 'bring the criminal law into disrepute'. The court must have regard for the age disparity between Dunbar and his victim and the appalling breach of trust that had been perpetrated. It would be 'wholly wrong to don blinkers and not have regard to the cover-up which was part and parcel of events'. It would also be wholly wrong to disregard Dunbar's attitude and demeanour during the trial. Mr Justice White said that these elements, coupled with the lack of remorse, previous bad character and lack of mitigating factors, meant that this case presented the rare and exceptional circumstance which warranted a life sentence for manslaughter.

Mr Justice White rejected Mr Grehan's application for leave to appeal the conviction and severity of sentence but allowed legal aid in the event of such an appeal.

Leeanna Mahon left the courtroom quickly, refusing to speak to reporters.

An hour after the sentence was imposed, Lisa Conroy, Dunbar's former wife and the mother of three of his daughters, spoke via telephone to Gerry Ryan on his RTÉ Radio 2 show from her home in London. She said she was relieved and pleased with the sentence, as she had thought he would get a lesser sentence for manslaughter. She believed that her former husband was evil incarnate. 'Have you seen the pictures in the papers? All you need to do is put a few horns on him. I feel safe now he has been given this sentence. I think he's got his just desserts. A life for a life. I think that was a good fair sentence. I feel this has provided closure.'

The reaction of Melissa's mother came two days later on the front page of the *News of the World* . 'I Wish Dunbar Had Killed Me Too' screamed the headline, accompanied by a photograph of Mary Mahon with her arm around her slain daughter. More family snaps were displayed on the inside pages as well as a picture of Mary clutching Melissa's favourite teddy bear. Mary told *News of the World* reporter Stephen Breen, 'It would have been better if he had strangled me as well. My life ended the day she died.'

In the article, the then 56 year old was described as being devastated by what had happened to Melissa and it was said that she had been living on medication since. She said Dunbar did not deserve to live and described him as 'evil, sick and deadly'. Mary told the newspaper that she believed Dunbar had killed Melissa when he found out she was pregnant with his child. She repeated what she had said in the victim impact statement about having attempted suicide and threatened that she would be successful at her next attempt and would return to haunt her daughter's killer. She said that all she had left of her youngest daughter was a teddy bear and some of her clothes, which she would never wash because they still held her smell. She said she was dreading the funeral which she believed would be even harder to cope with than the trial.

Mary said she did not blame her daughter for falling under Dunbar's spell. She had had her suspicions about what was going on but Melissa had assured her that her relationship with Dunbar was innocent. She was simply hanging around with his daughters. Mary said she was guilty of trusting her daughter. She believed Dunbar had brainwashed Melissa but she was not angry with her. Dunbar was a clever man who had preyed on the girl. Mary blamed herself for leaving London and returning to Sligo. She had nightmares about Dunbar and could not get the image of his smirking face out of her mind.

She also reacted to Mr Justice White's comments about the victim impact statement, saying that she was very disappointed with his remarks and would be happy to discuss them with him. He would see that she was not putting on an act. She said she would seek legal advice.

Melissa's father, Frederick, also spoke to the *News of the World* to defend himself against the accusations that he abused Melissa that had been made during the trial. Frederick accused Dunbar of concocting and spreading the allegations as a manoeuvre to cover his own tracks. The 70 year old said the accusations were a 'terrible lie' created by Dunbar. He hoped the man who 'slaughtered' his child would die in prison.

It emerged that some gardaí had doubted Melissa's accusations of sexual abuse at the hands of her father. A senior officer told the *Sunday Tribune* that Melissa was already wildly delusional by the time she had made the allegation and would have done anything to get away from her parents and move in with the Dunbars. Only Melissa knew the truth.

Melissa's remains were returned to her family for burial on 11 August 2009. It was thought that, in the event of an appeal by Dunbar, the funeral would have to be deferred but authorities released her remains.

Before the funeral, Mary Mahon told the *Sligo Weekender* that members of the family could at last pay their final respects to her daughter. Melissa was buried the following morning at Sligo Cemetery after a service at St Anne's Church in the town. Schoolfriends and teachers from the Mercy College formed a guard of honour as she was taken from the church. It had been a long and agonising wait for her family. The previous evening there had been a garda presence both outside and inside the church. Mary said, 'At least now we can give her a proper funeral and we will have a grave to go to. She was my baby girl and a part of me died with her. But at least we will have a form of closure now. We are happy to have her with us at last.'

It was later reported in the *Sunday World* that Mary did not manage to attend her daughter's funeral as she was unwell.

AFTERWORD

Over a week before Melissa was laid to rest, Dunbar's legal team lodged papers signalling his intention to appeal his conviction and sentence. At the time of writing, the grounds for his appeal had not been lodged and further charges of a nature which cannot be revealed for legal reasons were being prepared by the Director of Public Prosecutions.

Also at the time of writing, the Health Service Executive had stated that it could not yet say when the results of an investigation into its role in the case would be made available. A statement said:

> We can confirm that a Case Management Review has commenced. The review is chaired by an independent childcare consultant and two childcare specialists. Children First National Guidelines for the Protection of Welfare of Children 1999 mandates that such a review, as defined, is undertaken when a child dies whilst in the care of the Health Service Executive. The Health Service Executive had a significant level of involvement in the care of the late Melissa Mahon and the review team are not yet in a position to project when the report will be completed.